THE POWER OF PARTNERSHIP

Center for Engaged Learning
Open Access Book Series

Series editors, Jessie L. Moore and Peter Felten

The Center for Engaged Learning (CEL) Open Access Book Series features concise, peer-reviewed books (both authored books and edited collections) for a multi-disciplinary, international, higher education audience interested in research-informed engaged learning practices.

The CEL Open Access Book Series offers an alternate publishing option for high-quality engaged learning books that align with the Center's mission, goals, and initiatives, and that experiment with genre or medium in ways that take advantage of an online and open access format.

CEL is committed to making these publications freely available to a global audience.

Pedagogical Partnerships: A How-To Guide for Faculty, Students, and Academic Developers in Higher Education
Alison Cook-Sather, Melanie Bahti, and Anita Ntem

Forthcoming
Writing about Learning and Teaching in Higher Education
Mick Healey, Kelly E. Matthews, and Alison Cook-Sather
Summer 2020

The Power
of Partnership

Students, Staff, and Faculty
Revolutionizing Higher Education

Edited by Lucy Mercer-Mapstone and Sophia Abbot

Elon University Center for Engaged Learning
Elon, North Carolina
www.CenterforEngagedLearning.org

Series editors: Jessie L. Moore and Peter Felten
Copyeditor and designer: Jennie Goforth
Graphic illustrator: Sam Hester

Cataloging-in-Publication Data
Names: Mercer-Mapstone, Lucy | Abbot, Sophia
Title: The Power of Partnership: Students, Staff, and Faculty Revolutionizing Higher Education / Lucy Mercer-Mapstone and Sophia Abbot
Description: Elon, North Carolina : Elon University Center for Engaged Learning, [2020] | Series: Center for engaged learning open access book series | Includes bibliographical references and index.
Identifiers: LCCN 2019956342 | ISBN (PDF) 978-1-951414-02-3 | ISBN (pbk.) 978-1-951414-03-0 | DOI https://doi.org/10.36284/celelon.oa2
Subjects: LCSH: Teacher-student relationships | College teaching

To be part of a collection can be to become a collective.
(Sarah Ahmed, *On Being Included*)

~This book is dedicated to all our wonderful partners~

A NOTE FROM THE PUBLISHER

We are excited to share this edited collection as the second publication in our Center for Engaged Learning Open Access Book Series.

The Power of Partnership makes a significant, creative, and timely contribution to the scholarly literature on a growing trend in higher education—equitable collaborations among students, staff, and faculty in support of teaching and learning. These practices go by a number of (contested) names, including students-as-partners and student-faculty/staff partnership. As this book illustrates, this work can take a wide variety of forms, yet the shared principles underlying partnership have the potential to revolutionize higher education.

This collection includes 51 authors from around the globe, highlighting partnerships from different national and institutional contexts. As a result, readers will find relatable and adaptable—and perhaps provocative—ideas and strategies for their own partnerships and institutions.

To honor the diverse voices of the authors, we have preserved the variety of spellings and higher education terminology (e.g., American, Australian, etc.), but we have provided stylistic consistency by editing all the punctuation in accordance with our in-house style. We have created an online glossary to help readers understand terms that may be unfamiliar or that have different meanings in different countries.

Also included on the book's website (www.CenterForEngaged Learning.org/books/power-of-partnership) are additional supplemental resources, including videos and discussion questions.

Jessie L. Moore, series editor
Peter Felten, series editor
Jennie Goforth, managing editor

CONTENTS

A Partnership Origin [E-]Story

Lucy Mercer-Mapstone
Lecturer
University of Sydney
Australia

Sophia Abbot
Master's student
Elon University
United States

Dear Sophia,

I woke up at 4am last night with feelings of frustration and anger vibrating around my brain. I have been working on a thought piece on the importance of writing and publishing in non-academic genres that are accessible (and god forbid, enjoyable!) to staff *and* students. It's been a fun project—writing in a dialogue format which is new for me. It's incredibly liberating to be able to discuss ideas without the *blah blah blah* of "formal scholarship."

The irony of the situation though is that now that we have written this piece, it's been hard to find a journal that will accept such an outlandish genre. So, it was at 4am this morning (when all my most important fretting happens) that the lightbulb pinged. If it's so damn difficult to get this stuff published in mainstream formats, why don't I publish it myself? How amazing would it be to have a space for sharing our work together on partnership that isn't bogged down in the corset-like structures of academic "rigor"? A place where the emotion, joy, frustration, messiness—the *freedom*—of partnership doesn't need to be erased.

So, how about it? Want to write a book with me?

Talk soon.

–Lucy

★★★

Dear Lucy,

Yes, YES! You know, I've been feeling that frustration with scholarly writing for a while now. Every time I've thought about partnership lately, I think about the joy we've felt working together, the vulnerability, the frustration, the celebration, the radical energy (the fight-the-power excitement!) and I know that an empirical article just can't hold that.

I took a class on listening several years ago where the facilitators described our capacity to listen as bowls that adjust depending on our circumstances. Sometimes they're small but deep, and able to hold space for someone's very specific thoughts and emotions. Other times they're wide and shallow, and we can hold space for many different conversations and topics, but not with much depth. I think partnership makes space for both wide and deep listening and sharing, but most publishing venues are small and deep. We're forced to sieve away all of those beautiful emotions and ignore the little hiccups until we've got a few drops of partnership that we share out with the world barely resembling the vastness that really existed.

This is all to say, our book could be that bowl! Let's make space for experimenting with form and subject! Let's make sure this is accessible! Let's do it!

How should we get started?

~Sophia

★★★

Sophia,

Wow—a class on listening? How fantastic! I love that imagery of vessels that hold the breadth and depth of our practice. And you're so right—the places we publish either want that narrow depth or wide shallowness but rarely create space for both.

I'm so excited you'll collaborate on this. How should we start? Good question. Perhaps one place to dip our toe in would be to discuss the ideas that drive us to create this book?

I'll start us off. I guess for me it all started with genre. When I read the wide range of work on partnership certain words really jump out and resonate with me:

empowering

radical

inclusive

transformational

egalitarian

Sometimes as I read, I feel as if I have been punched in the gut, tears coming to my eyes when I see the powerful ways in which partnership work has impacted people. It connects to the deep sense of liberation I feel through my own partnerships. These instances are rare, though. Mostly, I am left wondering. Full of questions that I wish I could discuss with the authors—perhaps over coffee—where we could really delve down into the intricacies of the practices and ideas they have shared.

So, a recurring question I have is, *what genres lend themselves to sharing the intricate, complex, and relational realities of partnership?*

I don't believe it's the traditional, academic genres. I likened these in an earlier letter to a corset. Bone rigid, structured, tight, restrictive, and symbolically representative of certain power structures: exclusivity and enforced conformity. I frequently lament the sense of loss I feel when I try to fit/bind the complex nature of partnership within the boundaries of traditional academic formats. In the same way as wearing a corset, conforming to journal publishing standards often feels as if I have to erase my own shape, my embodied subjectivity, from my work—removing the bumps, the curves, the perfect imperfections.

I suppose I want this book to be a place where those bumps, curves, and imperfections are embraced and celebrated.

What about you?

–Lucy

Lucy,

Absolutely, yes—this is the place for "those bumps, curves, and imperfections": genre is a wonderful place to start. It's in those more dialogic moments with classmates, colleagues, and mentors that I've been brought to tears, reflecting on our vulnerability, expressing how empowered I've felt when working with a professor who truly saw and heard me. So, for me, genres that can really hold partnership are reflective, dialogic, open, expressive, and absolutely first-person. And I imagine there are other qualities and forms that I can't even imagine right now!

Another space I'm interested in that I think overlaps significantly is *language*. I'm thinking about how we talk about partnership to each other and to others, and I'm reminded of a small and wonderful partnership conference I was at last May in which we described partnership as "radical," "revolutionary," "transgressive"—words you highlighted as jumping out in the works you've read. Then I think about how I frame this to potential participants, as promoting engagement, building agency, encouraging reflection, improving learning. There are different levels to the language we use, and I'd love for this book to make space for the small-scale and short-term language alongside some of our lofty goals!

I'm also thinking about how we've just been referring to this as "partnership" with no subjects or objects, which would probably read as pretty vague to anyone outside of this! I should clarify: the partnership I've done has been an intensive, one-on-one, months- or year-long relationship between a professor and myself when I was an undergraduate. We came together to examine the shared space of the classroom and bring our different expertise (theirs in their content area, mine in being a student) to bear on making the classroom a more equitable and engaging learning environment. Other language I've heard used to describe this has been "student-faculty partnership" or "student-staff partnership" (that's a linguistic difference based on geography so to be clear, anyone employed in higher education could be considered "staff" and likewise, anyone studying, a "student"), as well as "students as partners," which I personally avoid using but acknowledge its value in being widely recognized.

What have your partnerships looked like? How do you talk about them?

~Sophia

Sophia,

Those are such important questions. And thank you for the timely reminder. Sometimes I get so *inside* my partnership bubble that I forget to be explicit about what I mean by "partnership." Perhaps because, even after many years, my understanding and "definition" is still evolving. That's a point that many have troubled in the partnership literature—that, as Healey, Flint, and Harrington (2014) discuss, a clear definition is often elusive because the work is so very personal and contextual.

Like you, my predominant forms of partnership have been small-scale: one-to-one or in small groups. These partnerships have continued over years though, rather than being short-term, and often span multiple projects rather than a single semester or course. Unlike you, mine have always taken place outside of the classroom, working on co-research projects focusing on partnership itself—a bit of a mind-bending meta-process at times! So, I think together the two of us bring real complementarity—covering a broad cross-section of spaces, places, and roles.

Many of my partnerships have actually been about introducing others to the idea or supporting others in developing their own practices through workshop facilitation. So, I have thought a lot about language and, as you rightly say, the absolute centrality of language in sharing and shaping our practices.

It's tricky. I agree with you in that having "students as partners" as an increasingly recognized term is useful for practitioners developing a shared language. I love that now on twitter I can search

#studentsaspartners and get a whole stream of thoughts and resources from all over the world.

For many years I accepted and adopted that term without a second thought. It places students at the heart of this movement, and maybe that's as it should be?

Recently though I spent some time thinking on that language—at a time when I was also immersing myself in various feminist works of literature. I discussed parallels between partnership and feminism with my mum, and we began to chew over the idea that perhaps that language is more troubling that we had initially thought. We wrote about it in 2017:

> Perhaps the student-centric focus [of "students as partners"] is a manifestation of the traditional power hierarchies of the institutions within which this movement is unfolding. Some of the feminist readings I have been devouring propose that there is intrinsic power in not being named—particularly within binaries. Wittig (1981) argues that there is only one gender: the feminine; that the "masculine" is not a gender, but the general or the norm and . . . does not need to be named but rather, assumed.

> Do you see the parallel? That "academics" go predominantly unnamed in [students as partners] terminology infers an implicit assumption that those academics do not need to be named because they are the general, the dominant, the norm against which the Other is defined. The way most of our labels begin with the word "student" might be argued to potentially mirror the fundamental power imbalance between those who are (implicitly) "allowing" such changes.

So, I suppose I have been opting more recently for "student-staff partnership" instead. I still don't feel particularly comfortable with that though because it reinforces the student/staff binary in a way that, for me, counters the aim of partnership: to break down divisions. And, as with all binaries, it also excludes the range of potential practitioners who do not feel they sit within either of those categories. That said, I don't actually have an alternative to offer other than to say that using simply "partnership" is what feels most right to me at the moment.

How do you think that this book might contribute to those complexities?

–Lucy

***

Lucy,

I've also been opting for "student-staff partnership" for clarity (though agree that the binarizing nature of it can be frustrating—obscuring the real messiness of roles we all inhabit!). In addition to your highlighting the absence of academics in "students as partners," I spoke with Alison Cook-Sather this summer (one of my partners and mentors!), and she mentioned hearing someone speak recently about "students as consultants." I immediately bristled at the term, and I couldn't quite figure out why at first. Then we realized: it reminded me of when children play pretend. It was as though I had been temporarily and maybe not fully *acting as* a consultant but not actually *being* a consultant. Students as partners echoes in a similar way to me: that students are temporarily acting in this role, without actually *being partners*.

And of course, that's not the intention, nor is it how we live it. There's amazing value—as you say—with having a broadly shared language. But I do believe deeply that words matter. I think it was Lacan who wrote about language speaking subjects into existence? This book can be a rich space for folks to use their preferred language, and perhaps grow our language to speak partnership into existence more richly and fully. I'd love for us to be able to share a range of ways of speaking.

Speaking of which, what exactly should our book be *about*?

~Sophia

***

Dear Sophia,

I had to pause numerous times when reading your last letter—so many powerful ideas that resonated with me. Especially that temporary nature of students *as* partners rather than *being* partners. It reminds me of recent discussions I have had with friends and colleagues Rachel Guitman and Anita Acai (another partnership of strong women from whom I find much inspiration!). We reflected on the way that institutions of learning often see students as transient rather than solid beings who establish foundations and remain part of the university community.

I have felt this sense of transience often in my university and, at times, that seems to get reflected into some partnerships. Not intentionally, perhaps, but the way we try to fit our partnership into existing structures makes it hard for those partnership spaces not to accidentally mimic the old ways of knowing and doing: where staff have a permanent seat at the table and students are invited in and then ushered out as useful. That all comes down to power, doesn't it?

I suppose that answers your question. I want this book to be about power. As Seale, Gibson, Haynes, and Potter wrote regarding student engagement, voice, and partnership, "if we continue to ignore issues of power and resistance, we will fall far short of the vision." I wholeheartedly agree. So, I imagine this book to focus on the examination and destabilization of traditional power hierarchies in higher education, not only through the content we include but through a book that is itself a deliberate act of disruption.

What about you? What do you think our book should be about?

–Lucy

Lucy,

Power should absolutely be a core theme. I find it's so present in all my interactions but especially when I'm negotiating a partnership—I constantly think about the different assumptions and expectations we're bringing. Deeply related to this is the intersecting identities we all bring to partnership. I'm thinking about how you and I have talked together about our shared identities: white, queer, cis-women. I'm thinking about the different ways we've negotiated spaces as a result of those identities, facing patriarchy and heterosexism while also acknowledging our privileges. Identity is key. And actually, when I wrote a review in 2017 of bell hooks' *Teaching to Transgress*, I noted something that I still think about constantly:

> Partnership has always been complicated by these politics of domination, but higher education's increasing diversification continues to raise new and different tensions. What is exciting—what I have begun to see in each of my partnerships and what hooks helps us to imagine—is that partnership also opens the possibility of radical transformation through these connections across difference.

Perhaps rather than focus solely on identity, though it is so present, we might focus on that radically transformative space: the intersections and connections made possible through partnership.

Am I missing anything?

~Sophia

Sophia,

I know we have talked a lot about the transformative potential of partnership and the personal growth we have each been through as a result. I wonder whether that might be a theme that opens up the book to some more context-specific discussions?

Ruth and Mick Healey recently wrote that when it comes to questions about partnership, the answer is most often, "it depends." They say that "there is a need to identify the structural, temporal, and personal dimensions that define the context. . . . We cannot begin to understand the processes and outcomes of specific partnerships without taking account of the context in which they operate."

Perhaps we can honor that necessary context by inviting people to share their stories of individual or institutional growth through partnership? I find those sorts of reflection so powerful. For example, in 2018, Paul Wynkoop, a student partner at Haverford College in the United States, wrote:

> Given my identity as a white male, I felt as though I came to understand more deeply [through partnership] just how crucial giving space to people of other, often marginalized identities is. I had long considered myself someone who understood when it was appropriate for me to talk and when it wasn't, but hearing just how important it was to other students . . . that there be space for all identities made inclusion an even more important principle I aimed to enact and achieve. This led me to be even more conscious of my presence within my own classrooms and how I interacted with other students.

It is this kind of deep reflection on personal awareness and transformation that I would love to see shared on these pages.

–Lucy

***

Lucy,

Yes! I totally agree. So where to now? While I think we could fill a whole book with *our* thoughts on partnership, there are so many phenomenal people thinking and working in this space! Let's include as many of those voices as we can. We could invite those potential authors to play with genre as much as they like and just see what happens!

What do you think?

~Sophia

***

Dear Sophia,

Let's get started!

–Lucy

Dear Readers,

We hope that, as you've read through these letters, you've gained a sense of the organic symbioses that birthed this book. We also hope to have shared our aspirations, joy, and excitement in putting together this collection, especially with such an invigorating melting-pot of authors.

We are thrilled the following chapters contain works from fifty-one authors—twenty-three students, twenty-six staff and faculty, and two academic researchers—hailing from twenty-one institutions across six countries. Chapters are organized to address three themes:

Power and Politics
how power and politics influence and shape partnerships
from inside and out

Intersections
the overlaps and interplay between partnership and its intersections with different theories, pedagogies, cultures, and identities

Growing Partnership
growth through and of partnership in different contexts at
personal, classroom, and institutional levels

Authors truly embraced our call to bend or break traditional academic molds and have shared their thoughts through essays, poetry, dialogue, manifesto, art, and . . . Each section has been depicted using glorious graphic illustration by the talented Sam Hester.

We hope this collection will provide you with as much inspiration, provocation, and nourishment as it has done us.

On that note, we dedicate this book to you—our fellow radical partnership practitioners alongside whom we find such liberation.

Yours,

Lucy & Sophia

References

Abbot, Sophia. 2017. "Book Review of Teaching to Transgress: Education as the Practice of Freedom." *International Journal for Students as Partners* 1 (2): 1-2. https://doi.org/10.15173/ijsap.v1i2.3230.

Healey, Mick, Abbi Flint, and Kathy Harrington. 2014. *Engagement through Partnership: Students as Partners in Learning and Teaching in Higher Education*. York, UK: Higher Education Academy. https://www.advance-he.ac.uk/knowledge-hub/engagement-through-partnership-students-partners-learning-and-teaching-higher.

Healey, Mick, and Ruth Healey. 2018. "'It Depends': Exploring the Context-dependent Nature of Students as Partners Practices and Policies." *International Journal for Students as Partners* 2 (1): 1-10. https://doi.org/10.15173/ijsap.v2i1.3472.

Mercer-Mapstone, Lucy, and Gina Mercer. 2017. "A Dialogue between Partnership and Feminism: Deconstructing Power and Exclusion in Higher Education." *Teaching in Higher Education* 23 (1): 137-43. https://doi.org/10.1080/13562517.2017.1391198.

Seale, Jane, Suanne Gibson, Joanna Haynes, and Alice Potter. 2015. "Power and resistance: Reflections on the rhetoric and reality of using participatory methods to promote student voice and engagement in higher education." *Journal of Further and Higher Education* 39 (4): 534-52. https://doi.org/10.1080/0309877X.2014.938264.

Wynkoop, Paul. 2018. "My Transformation as a Partner and a Learner." *Teaching and Learning Together in Higher Education* 23: 1-5. https://repository.brynmawr.edu/tlthe/vol1/iss23/4.

(Re)Envisioning Partnership

Lucy Mercer-Mapstone
Lecturer
University of Sydney
Australia

Sophia Abbot
Master's student
Elon University
United States

In short, we have many questions.
What do we do when we use the same terms without realizing
we are talking past each other?
We re-examine?
The single story of partnership could be a barrier to growth.

What *is* partnership?

Scholars use many names.
Our space is probably most familiar to you as
"students as partners" or "student-staff partnership."
The language startles:
it invites dialogue, as metaphors do.
It asks us to *unlearn* what we think we know.

Machinations of higher education are always governed by politics.
The -isms are well documented and
hard to ignore.
Partnership is a political process,
questioning taken-for-granted ways,
working against the grain.

Here, it's different.
Partnership opens up new spaces—
spaces in the margin,
counter-spaces that challenge;
collaborative
equitable
relationships
in teaching and learning.
Aspirational, values-based,
highlighting the collocations
academic selves / student selves,
      past selves / future selves,
we've all *been* students.
Partnership provokes us,
destabilizing neat categorizations
that abstract us.
Partnership makes us human again.

The ambiguity of partnership opens our eyes:
      pushes us to accept discomfort,
      offers a new language, a new lens to explore,
      writes new rules for the classroom
            exercise patience
            be open-minded
            fully understand
    be playful in academic spaces
            be joyful.
  You choose who you're going to be in partnership.
  A way of being in the academy: *We are no longer acting.*

We must take seriously multiple sites of power;
we navigate difficult terrain.
This requires careful attention by all.
    I was not always met with understanding,
    I developed resilience through these resistances.

This resilience allowed me to push back.

But how do we engage in partnership *meaningfully*?
We have to be ready for unexpected, sudden branchings:
"Can students truly be equal
        when power, privilege, and status are inscribed?"
"Are we unintentionally reinforcing exclusive beliefs?"
"I wonder about the missionary, civilizing tones
        of bringing 'resistant' students into the fold."
Does this sound familiar to you?
Why do you think that is?
We persist nevertheless,
        the urgency, weariness, hope, and hesitation.
        Some of us turned inside out,
        all of us disheveled and disoriented.
This is a place in which we stretch ourselves,
in which we rely on one another to pull us in new directions,
in which we are all equally twisted up.

"Ako" [Māori]:
both to teach and to learn;
this was our understanding of partnership.
Students astonished that staff seek their perspectives,
staff re-energized by the thoughtfulness of students,
we became cohesive:
transformed by authentic encounters.

Partnerships allow us to aspire:
We listen anew to each voice
to know we would never know once and for all.

Our wonderful series editors, Jessie Moore and Peter Felten, suggested in early feedback that we offer an "updated definition of partnership and context for partnership work—what do readers who are coming to partnership for the first time need to know?"

We struggled with this for a while—how could we define partnership in new ways that didn't step on the toes of all the wonderful ways it has been defined before? There have been so many fantastic overviews and recounts of partnership in previous works that inspire and resonate, many of which are drawn on in the following chapters, providing a foundation for this book.

We decided to offer, instead of an updated definition, the (re)envisioning which we shared with you above. Keeping in the (non)tradition of this collection in inviting creative genres, this (re)envisioning was created through poetic transcription. Poetic transcription is a process of re-presenting data in the form of poetry where the words of a dataset are reshaped into poems with minor textual changes (for example, changes in tense). We learned of this practice through and were inspired by the powerful poetic transcription by Isabella Lenihan-Ikin, Brad Olsen, Kathryn Sutherland, Emma Tennent, and Marc Wilson in chapter 5. This form of re-presenting results makes room for "the shapes of inter-subjectivity, and examining issues of power and authority . . . inclusive of emotional reactions as well as analytical descriptions" (Glesne 1997, 204). Appropriate, given the topic, don't you think?

The "dataset" we used to create the above (re)envisioning were the words of our authors in this edited collection—drawing on and riffing off their insightfulness. In this way, we incorporated the voices and wisdom of not only the fifty authors writing here, but also of the authors who came before us whose voices powerfully shaped our partnership thinking, writing, and practices.

This poetic transcription of partnership touches on many of the current themes and contexts of partnership work and scholarship. The first and second stanzas raise the multitude of questions which seems to be a facet of the field—what is partnership, what do we call it, and how do we talk about it? Having a shared language is critical for individuals to feel that they belong to a community as well as for movements to have a common point of reference (Palmer 1992). Sometimes, that language raises further questions—as in the fifth line of stanza one where Sasha Mathrani, drawn from chapter 10, articulates the limitations we self-impose when we hold too dearly to a "single story of partnership." Indeed, it is in the iterative reflection on how language shapes our partnerships that we come to learn more deeply about ourselves, our assumptions, and our field—as is discussed in numerous chapters (3, 7, 8, 9, 10, 11, and 13) of this collection.

The third stanza broadens to consider the sectorial context within which partnerships happen. Partnership scholars often position the practice of partnership as radical in the ways it "works against the grain" (as described by Kelly Matthews in chapter 7) in an environment which increasingly is embracing neoliberalism, managerialism, and academic capitalism. Rachel Guitman and Beth Marquis in chapter 9, in describing that context, argue that partnership thus can become a political process which, in risk-averse environments of higher education, ironically, can bring more significant risks for practitioners and practices—such as the risk of false expectations established in empty partnership rhetoric described by Rachel Guitman, Anita Acai, and Lucy Mercer-Mapstone in chapter 3.

Stanza four conceptualizes partnership, where "Here, it's different" (poignantly articulated by Rumy Begum in chapter 14). As Abbi Flint calls it in chapter 11, this "space in the margins" lets in all sorts of rich juxtapositions between (our/other) selves—illustrated in chapter 8 by Amani Bell, Steph Barahona, and Bonnie Stanway. Tai Peseta, Jenny Pizzica, Ashley Beathe, Chinnu Jose, Racquel Lynch, Marisse Manthos, Kathy Nguyen, and Hassan Raza in chapter 6 recount how, as we rehumanize within these spaces, the "literature is flooded with case after case from around the world of students, staff, practices, and institutions being transformed by authentic encounters of pedagogical partnership." The body of evidence seems to be swelling into an unequivocal peak.

This swell flows into the fifth stanza, into the personal parts of partnership—what we, as individuals, gain when our eyes are opened to the generative "ambiguity of partnership," as described by Anita Ntem in chapter 13. Iteratively challenging and reconstituting our roles and identities (Amani Bell, Steph Barahona, and Bonnie Stanway, chapter 8), partnership experiences present a troublesome but potentially transformational threshold which, as we step, leap, bound (or trip) over, gives us a new "way of being in the academy" (Abbi Flint, chapter 11) meaning that, perhaps, we are no longer acting (Anne Bruder, chapter 15).

Stanza six dives into the turbulent issues of power where Roselynn Verwoord and Heather Smith (chapter 1) urge us to consider how our multiple social locations—and the intersections between different locations—inscribe us and our partnerships with potentially insurmountable asymmetries. As Isabella Lenihan-Ikin and colleagues discuss in chapter 5, this omnipresent power raises tensions between equality and equity, which play out in partnership. These tensions are met with calls to *unlearn* in chapters 3 and 7—asking us to question what we know, hang our assumptions out for examination in the light of a plurality of knowledges. Critical engagement with, and dialogue about, such differences may be the most challenging aspect of partnership work but also the facet that potentially offers the highest rewards.

The seventh stanza speaks powerfully to the very real and messy realities of what it means to engage in partnership *meaningfully*. This and other gritty questions are posed here by Roselyn and Heather, and Sean Wilson, Julie Phillips, Helen Meskhidze, Claire Lockard, Peter Felten, Susannah McGowan, and Stephen Bloch-Schulman (in chapters 1 and 2, respectively). These questions won't go away as the partnership field progresses—there are no simple (re)solutions. But perhaps that insolvable nature of partnership is what keeps us coming back for more, continuously tying ourselves into human knots which, as Anne so eloquently describes in chapter 15, pull us, stretch us, turn us inside out.

Our final stanza speaks to the sense of cohesion we have all felt when a partnership bears fruit: when we pluck the benefits in and of the process and aspire to continue to learn in the liminal partnership space of, as Alison Cook-Sather puts it in chapter 10, never knowing once and for all.

References

Glesne, Corrine. 1997. "That Rare Feeling: Re-presenting Research Through Poetic Transcription." *Qualitative Inquiry* 3, no. 2 (June): 202-21. https://doi.org/10.1177/107780049700300204.

Palmer, Parker J. 1992. "Divided No More." *Change: The Magazine of Higher Learning* 24, no. 2 (March/April): 10-17. https://doi.org/10.1080/00091383.1992.9937103.

SECTION ONE

POWER AND POLITICS

Re-envisioning the Academy

Speaking Up against "The Single Story"

Chng Huang Hoon
Associate professor
National University of Singapore
Singapore

Since hearing the Nigerian author Chimamanda Ngozi Adichie's TED Talk *The Danger of a Single Story* (2009), I have been repeatedly reminded of the need for us to guard against dominant narratives. It would, therefore, be naïve to attempt any story about staff-student partnership without first facing up to the *one* dominant story that has been circulating in the academy—that such partnerships are either difficult to forge, or if they exist, they can take only one form, with staff leading students. This section on *Power and Politics* addresses these important and difficult issues from five different angles. Authors deploy different genres in the form of two dialogic pieces (chapters 1 and 4), two pieces of narrative prose (chapters 2 and 3), and a final poetic transcription (chapter 5). The different linguistic forms aptly capture the many "colors" of partnerships, illustrating the complexities of discoursing about this dynamic human interaction. This book as a whole and the chapters in this section collectively challenge the current "way of being in the academy" (chapter 11, Flint) and drives home the point that "the single story of partnership could [and would] be a barrier to growth" (chapter 10, Mathrani).

The two important strands of power and politics are laid delightfully bare through honest discussions and critiques by the authors of each chapter. In their poetic (re)envisioning of partnership in the introduction, Lucy Mercer-Mapstone and Sophia Abbot set the stage for this book with the many questions posed by authors, the most fundamental being "What *is* partnership?" (from chapter 13, Ntem). Among the many statements Lucy and Sophia quote in their poem, what I found most enlightening were the following two timely reminders: "We've all *been* students" (from chapter 8, Bell, Barahona, and Stanway) and "Partnership makes us human again" (based on the ideas of chapter 7, Matthews). These words push us to rethink the challenges surrounding staff-student partnership and to find a productive resolution, even if it means that we will need to rework the practice of our academy and cease treating student partners as "naïve voices" (chapter 5, Lenihan-Ikin et al.), or as "novelties" (chapter 2, Wilson et al.). In confronting power and politics, I urge all of us to call up our empathetic memory and understanding of what it means to be students, and to center the humanity that binds us, regardless of our ascribed identities and the roles we play in our institutions.

A message I believe worth highlighting here is one offered in chapters 2 and 3 about what established members in the academy *can* do. Both chapters allude to the role—and I will add, the responsibility—that can be actively assumed by "the powerful insiders in SoTL" (chapter 2, Wilson et al.), that "those already within the partnership community [must] increasingly look outward . . . [to] reach out and extend the boundaries of our practices, our discussions, and our networks to welcome newcomers with an ethos of absolute inclusivity" (chapter 3, Guitman, Acai, and Mercer-Mapstone). As Wilson et al. put it, "Active ally-ship is central." I believe wholeheartedly that we must *intentionally* include individuals and groups so that we do not *unintentionally* exclude them. An attitude of generosity and advocacy towards others newer to the practice is crucial if we wish to enrich the academy to grow and to improve.

Another kind of "ally-ship" is mapped out in chapter 4 by Abbi Flint and Hannah Goddard, who bring us into the terrain of student representation systems like student unions and discuss how they relate to the academic community. This chapter takes the form of a dialogic exchange between an educational developer/researcher and a student engagement professional and presents the situational reality of student unions as both independent of and interdependent with the institutions of which they are a part. The nature of such partnerships presents a curious situation where reps experience a kind of split reality in which power remains elusive because they are, to rephrase Roselynn Verwoord and Heather Smith, hampered by the ever-present specter of the student-staff hierarchy (chapter 1). If we work on reducing and dissolving barriers, or, if we cannot eliminate them, then actively backgrounding power differentials, student reps can be better empowered to perform their role. The position we choose to adopt, the openness and willingness of spirit, our conscious decision not to involve ourselves in ethnocentric thinking, and the reflexive stance that we must bring into our practice—all captured by the P.O.W.E.R framework in chapter 1 by Roselynn Verwoord and Heather Smith—will go a long way in promoting "ally-ship" and equity in our relationships with professional peers, students included.

The final chapter in this section, by Isabella Lenihan-Ikin et al., takes us out of the idea of partnership as a political process into the realm of civic space to, as they say, "investigate how best to encourage university-community partnerships through civically engaged curricula" and to view "the university itself as a civic space" (chapter 5)—a space of inclusivity and frank engagement, a sanctioned safe space that allows for collaboration and free exchange. Though this may sound idealistic, we should remind ourselves that, ideologically, academic institutions should be built on principles like freedom of knowledge pursuit and exchange, rather than as political arenas that favor hierarchy over partnerships. Our institutions ought to be spaces where we critically deconstruct normativity and be vigilant in asking, *Well, is this normal? Should it be this way? Why should it not be this way?*

It should come naturally to us to relate to one another as equals, as humans, as authentic voices, rather than as individuals on different sides of an unscaleable fence. I do not believe in "neutral spaces" (chapter 5, Isabella Lenihan-Ikin et al.) or in power being eradicated, but I do have faith in a humanity based on shared citizenship, community, and collaboration. I have learned a great deal from the generosity of the authors who have taken the time to explicate the different ways in which partnership can be forged and how power can be alleviated. I applaud them for resisting the single story of partnership and, in their own way, advocating for *ako* (chapter 5, Isabella Lenihan-Ikin et al.)—teaching and learning, together.

CHAPTER 1

The P.O.W.E.R. Framework

Power Dimensions Shaping Students as Partners Processes

Roselynn Verwoord
PhD candidate
University of British Columbia
Canada

Heather Smith
Professor
University of N. British Columbia
Canada

We have explored the ways various dimensions of power play through our partnerships over several projects. With each partnership the process can take different shapes, and as such, we navigate various dimensions of power. Building on our work with Angela Kehler (Kehler, Verwoord, and Smith 2017), we present a conceptual framework using the word P.O.W.E.R. to foster reflection on some of the power dimensions that can shape partnerships. We engage in a dialogue about the P.O.W.E.R. framework and use auto-ethnography and narrative dialogue as a method to give expression to our reflections. We want to introduce ourselves before we discuss the framework because positionality is central to our analysis.

Roselynn: I come to the partnership field wearing many "hats." These hats include a student "hat" (as a PhD candidate), an instructor "hat" (in various teacher and adult education programs), and a curriculum consultant "hat" (as a staff person situated in a university teaching and learning center). My experiences wearing these hats shape how I view and understand student-staff partnership. To use Britzman's (1997) words, through my multiple hats, I experience the "tangles of implication" (32).

My interest in partnership is grounded in my commitment to education as a tool for social change. Often, I explore questions such as: What does it mean to engage students as equal partners in activities to improve teaching and learning? Can students *truly* be equal when issues of power, privilege, and status are inscribed in the terms "student" and "faculty"— terms that necessarily shape the ways we interact with and understand relationships and activities within education? I operate from the standpoint that partnership can be a positive experience. But how do we engage in partnership *meaningfully*? What are some of the challenges of creating authentic partnerships? How do we navigate these barriers while being mindful of power, privilege, and social location?

Heather: I'm a critical feminist with a PhD in political science, and a professor of global and international studies at the University of Northern British Columbia (UNBC). My area of expertise is gender and Canadian foreign policy. I'm also the former director of the Centre for Teaching, Learning, and Technology at UNBC. I too wear many hats.

Synthesizing my critical feminist approach and the students as partners model has resulted in questions that center on power in everyday practices and processes. We must take seriously the multiple sites of power in partnerships and interrogate how power manifests. Like Roselynn, I wonder about claims to equality in a system built on hierarchies, the power of labeling "student" and "faculty" in the model itself, and the sometimes missionary and civilizing tones of bringing "resistant" students into the fold. In short, I have many questions.

How we define/understand partnership

There are varying definitions and interpretations of partnership given the increasing interest in the field and corresponding growth in published literature. Drawing on Healey, Flint, and Harrington (2014, 2016), we define partnership as "a specific form of student engagement . . . a way of doing things, rather than an outcome in itself" (2014, 2). Partnership requires that we navigate the difficult terrain of power hierarchies. This necessitates careful thought and attention by all partners.

Current literature on power and partnership

There is existing scholarship that raises important questions related to power and partnership (see Bovill et al. 2016; Cook-Sather 2007; Cook-Sather and Alter 2011; Felten et al. 2013; Mihans, Long, and Felten 2008). There is acknowledgment within the literature of the power inherent in the creation of students as partners practices (Bovill et al. 2016; Seale et al. 2015) and the impact of "power differentials in terms of authority, institutional status, and expertise" (Weller et al. 2013, 11). The power related to the socially constructed roles of student, faculty, or staff and how those roles are dynamic, fluid, often overlapping, and context specific is another central theme (Kehler, Verwoord, and Smith 2017; Weller et al. 2013).

The power of non-action (or what is often called resistance), misrepresentation (Weller et al. 2013), and silences (Smith 2017) are themes that arise in some literature, often in relation to students. We believe resistance or withholding by students is an act of power and agency. We need to pay attention to silence, be mindful of how we interpret silence, and respect students "for their astuteness in appreciating the reality of the relationship they have with lecturers—a relationship in which they, as students, are perhaps minor rather than major stakeholders" (Seale et al. 2015, 548). We do not underestimate the ability of those labeled "student" to appreciate and navigate power (Cates, Madigan, and Reitenauer 2018; Dwyer 2018; Silvers 2016; van Dam 2016).

As Kelly Matthews (2017, 3) has recently observed "power, whether discussed or left unspoken, is always a factor in [students as partners] interactions" and we must be attentive to both conscious and unconscious habits and behaviors. One way to ensure attentiveness to partnership practices and to remain mindful of our conscious and unconscious habits and behaviors is through ongoing reflective practice as individuals and teams. Relationship building, conversation, and dialogue are all practices central to the partnership literature (see Allin 2014).

The P.O.W.E.R. Framework

Our framework seeks to prompt reflection on some of the dimensions shaping power relations in partnership. We emphasize the role of the individual within partnership to help others develop or enhance their awareness of power hierarchies. We believe that, with awareness, individuals can make an informed choice to challenge the reproduction of power hierarchies.

Critical educational theorists (Freire 2002; Giroux 1997; Shor 1992), feminist scholars (Enloe 1996, 2004; Sylvester 2009; Zalewski 1996, 2006), and Indigenous scholars (Battiste 2000; Denzin, Lincoln, and Tuhiwai Smith 2008; Tuhiwai Smith 1999) inform our understanding of power hierarchies as gendered, racialized, heteronormative, class-based, and ableist. As white, settler, Canadian, cis-gendered women, we acknowledge the biases in our scholarly gaze based on our positionality. Given the centrality of context, we take seriously the calls from the Truth and Reconciliation Commission of Canada (2015, 7) to engage in "education for reconciliation," which, for us, means engaging in decolonization through our work to the extent possible given our positionality. Thus, our framework takes an intersectional approach to theorizing power.

Positionality is the ability to consider one's position and social location and to view these aspects as relational where context and aspects of our identities (gender, race, class, etc.) are fluid and changing (Alcoff 1988). Positionality involves individuals taking up a position within a context and constructing meaning from this position (Alcoff 1988). Positionality in partnership involves individuals asking themselves questions including: What subject position (position shaped by discourse or ways of thinking) am I taking up? Based on the position and social locations we occupy, how much power do I have in this partnership? How much power do others have?

Openness is the desire to explore what might be possible. In partnership, openness involves asking questions about the purpose, goals, visions, and desires that partners have for partnership. Openness requires all partners to reflect on being open to others' ideological assumptions, to learn from multiple perspectives, to be vulnerable, and to say, "I don't know." Openness involves embracing the diverse, messy, and exhilarating processes of partnership. Openness is demonstrated by asking questions such as: What are my goals for participating in this partnership? What are my partners' goals? To what extent am I open to the process of partnership and all that it could entail in terms of my own learning and vulnerability? To what extent are my partners open to the process of partnership? How will I know if I and others are being open throughout the partnership?

Willingness to invest time involves the concept of temporality, which can be understood as past, present, and future, as well as space, place, and being. It involves: determining how much time one has to participate in partnership or to engage in relationship building; reflecting on one's past and present experiences with partnership; and determining to what extent participating is a priority. Determining one's willingness to invest time in the process involves asking questions like: Am I/will I be an important stakeholder in this partnership? Does the partnership process attend to aspects that are important to me? How might participating in this partnership attend to my hopes? Am I/will I make the time to build the relationships that are essential to this process?

Ethnocentricity is having the attitude that one's own group is superior. In partnership, ethnocentricity can take the form of partners making assumptions about each other. Whether intentional or not, making assumptions about various groups can limit what is possible. Developing an awareness of ethnocentricity involves individuals asking questions like: Does this partnership imply that anyone who disagrees with what is proposed is wrong? Does the partnership acknowledge that there are multiple ways of looking at the same issue? Am I making assumptions about certain groups of people or individuals, based on a homogenized label such as "faculty," "student," or "staff"?

Reflexivity is the ability to recognize how individuals are shaped by and can shape their environment; how the self and other exist in relation. Reflexivity supports individuals to "open new ways of addressing . . . long-standing questions of how and what we can legitimately take ourselves to know and what the limitations of our knowledge are" (Davies et al. 2004, 364). Reflexivity in partnerships involves individuals asking questions like: How are my interests and actions being shaped, supported, or limited by the interests and actions of others? How are my actions or inactions shaping the experience of myself or others? How are my actions or inactions shaping or being shaped by the environment within which we are situated?

This framework provides a tool for ongoing reflective practice as individuals involved in students as partners practice. It also provides prompts for conversations that can be held between partners.

Dialogue about the Framework

To breathe life into our P.O.W.E.R. framework, this next section is a conversation about how aspects of the framework connect to our experiences navigating power in partnerships.

Heather: Ros, how has *positionality* played a role in your partnership experiences?

Roselynn: Conversations about positionality often don't happen, and so we don't unpack our positionality. For example, I recall a situation where someone made assumptions about levels of knowledge and positioned my knowledge as superior, given my status as a PhD candidate. A discussion about levels of privilege hadn't occurred before this situation. We could have used this opportunity to consciously talk about how positionality influences all aspects of our partnerships.

Heather: Your response raises questions about the subject position and how partnerships are often created around roles. Our experience shows that partnership requires attentiveness to assumptions about what is known and assumptions about scholarly practice. You engage in a conversation and are used to ways of acting and being, and you might not always take the time to explain your assumptions. If we are not mindful of that, we can silence people.

Silencing can happen through our everyday practice. In a world full of acronyms, for example, we need to ensure everyone is aware of what the acronyms mean because, otherwise, our conversational shorthand becomes exclusive. Similarly, in the desire to "get things done," we can overlook the vital need to check in. Checking in brings our voices back to the process.

Roselynn: Yes, focusing on roles reinforces subject positions. Perhaps our more fluid and contextual definition of positionality sheds light on the importance of having conversations about power and privilege from the start of a partnership. What has *openness* meant in your partnership experiences?

Heather: Two elements come to mind: wonder and harm. Wonder can occur when we are open to and focused on the process, not just the product. I had an experience where I was ready to work with a student on a project, and her insights totally flipped the project on its head in the most amazing way. That moment of wonder wouldn't have happened if I hadn't been open to the process.

Reciprocal openness must involve recognition by partners that in openness we can be harmed. Honestly, it's hard to discuss harm in any detail because I feel an ethical obligation to keep private the depth of some of our experiences. Let me just say, in my efforts to challenge my roles and be open, I've sometimes felt more vulnerable and exposed.

Roselynn: For sure . . . openness requires shifting away from the social, cultural, and institutional norms that individuals operate within and exploring new ways of doing things. We need to be open to thinking about positionality and willing to invest *time* in the process. We also need to ask ourselves questions about these aspects up front because, as you mention, the potential for harm is significant.

Heather: It seems as though there is a tension between the possibility that openness can provide and the potential for harm that can occur in the process of being open. That's tricky. So, Ros, how has a *willingness to invest time* in the process been a consideration in your partnerships?

Roselynn: In a new partnership, this has to do with who is asking me to invest in the process and what kinds of approaches they are taking to partnership. For example, is it a collaborative approach or a more traditional, roles-based approach? It also involves thinking about who I am and how I might contribute to the partnership, which connects to relationality. In an existing partnership, my willingness to invest time in the process is fluid and can change depending on how the partnership is unfolding. This reinforces the notion of power and links to the concept of individual agency—where individuals can use their power and agency to make choices about their participation.

Heather: When I think about time, I think about it in a neoliberal sense where time is seen as a commodity. Although I don't like thinking of time in this way, the reality is that post-secondary institutions have finite resources, and we are socialized to view resources like that. It's clear to me that, because partnership is relational, it takes dedicated time; however, how is one's time valued? Are all partners being rewarded for their time?

Roselynn: It's interesting that we touched on different aspects of time. Perhaps that's because we occupy different positions and social locations. What are your thoughts on *ethnocentricity* in partnership?

Heather: I've often had moments of surprise in my partnerships where I realized how deeply embedded I am in Western, masculinist norms and values. Working with Indigenous students and elders always provides me with moments of surprise about how colonial my practices can be. But these moments are valuable because they remind me that we need to be deeply mindful in partnership of how race and gender are normalized and how these social demographics are linked to power. We need to see power hierarchies as socially constructed roles that come with histories. Those histories are given expression through, for example, pictures of Queen Elizabeth in our public spaces—pictures which represent a colonial history to Canada's Indigenous peoples.

Roselynn: I think about how post-secondary institutions operate based on a Eurocentric model of education where we privilege Western knowledges and practices. What might it look like to decolonize partnership given that it is a practice and ethos currently situated within a Eurocentric system of education?

Heather: We both emphasize the importance of shifting away from ways of being where the privileged often possess more power. How has *reflexivity* been important in your partnerships?

Roselynn: Reflexivity invites me to explore questions that connect to positionality, such as: Who am I? Who am I in relation to others? What insights/learnings am I gleaning from my relationality to others? What am I going to do differently based on my insights from my partners? These questions are complex: everything that we say or don't say or do or don't do contributes to partners' experiences in the partnership.

Heather: As someone who can overthink things, I feel my own reflexivity needs to be balanced with mechanisms for feedback in partnership. And this feedback needs to be coupled with action. I believe partnerships can be transformative, but we need to take our collective reflections and manifest them in our actions.

Roselynn: Your point about the need for feedback and dialogue to work through the messiness of partnership is important. In a recent partnership, one partner was engaging in more work than others and was feeling frustrated. We engaged in some heartfelt conversations about expectations and the importance of creating space to share our frustrations. Feedback and dialogue were important. I also think it's great that the two of us just engaged in a reflective dialogue about the components of the P.O.W.E.R. framework as a way of working through the messiness of our own experiences of partnership.

Concluding Reflections

Power is central to students as partners relationships and practices. We need to move beyond acknowledging power and begin to unpack it—to work collaboratively to identify contextual sites and sources of power. The P.O.W.E.R. framework is a starting point. As in our own dialogue, partners can use the framework to foster rich conversations and to help explore the micro (everyday) and sometimes hidden aspects of power in partnership practices. Our conversations have shown us that reflection about the dimensions of power helps us navigate partnerships in ways that are thoughtful and respectful while simultaneously building trust. We continue to learn from each other because "we are the process" (Kehler, Verwoord, and Smith 2017, 1).

Reflection Questions for Readers

- How do you currently address sites of power in your partnerships?
- How might the P.O.W.E.R framework be helpful in your partnerships? How might you introduce it?
- How would you expand the P.O.W.E.R. framework?

References

Alcoff, Linda. 1988. "Cultural Feminism Versus Post-Structuralism: The Identity Crisis in Feminist Theory." *Signs* 13, no. 3 (Spring): 405-36. http://www.jstor.org/stable/3174166.

Allin, Linda. 2014. "Collaboration Between Staff and Students in the Scholarship of Teaching and Learning: The Potential and the Problems." *Teaching and Learning Inquiry* 2 (1): 95-102. https://doi.org/10.2979/teachlearninqu.2.1.95.

Battiste, Marie, ed. 2000. *Reclaiming Indigenous Voice and Vision.* Vancouver: UBC Press.

Bovill, Cathy, Alison Cook-Sather, Peter Felten, Luke Millard, and Niamh Moore-Cherry. 2016. "Addressing Potential Challenges in Co-creating Learning and Teaching: Overcoming Resistance, Navigating Institutional Norms, and Ensuring Inclusivity in Student-Staff Partnerships." *Higher Education* 71, no. 2 (February): 195-208. https://doi.org/10.1007/s10734-015-9896-4.

Britzman, Deborah. 1997. "The Tangles of Implication." *Qualitative Studies in Education* 10, (1): 31-37. https://doi.org/10.1080/095183997237386.

Cates, Rhiannon, Mariah Madigan, and Vicki Reitenauer. 2018. "'Locations of Possibility': Critical Perspectives on Partnership."

International Journal of Students as Partners 2 (1): 33-46. https://doi.org/10.15173/ijsap.v2i1.3341.

Cook-Sather, Alison. 2007. "Resisting the Impositional Potential of Student Voice Work: Lessons for Liberatory Educational Research from Poststructuralist Feminist Critiques of Critical Pedagogy." *Discourse* 28, no. 3 (September): 389-403. https://doi.org/10.1080/01596300701458962.

Cook-Sather, Alison, and Zanny Alter. 2011. "What Is and What Can Be: How a Liminal Position Can Change Learning and Teaching in Higher Education." *Anthropology & Education Quarterly* 42 (1): 37-53. https://doi.org/10.1111/j.1548-1492.2010.01109.x.

Davies, Bronwyn, Jenny Browne, Susanne Gannon, Eileen Honan, Cath Laws, Babette Mueller-Rockstroh, and Eva Bendix Peterson. 2004. "The Ambivalent Practices of Reflexivity." *Qualitative Inquiry* 10, no. 3 (June): 360-389. https://doi.org/10.1177/1077800403257638.

Denzin, Norman, Yvonna Lincoln, and Linda Tuhiwai Smith, eds. 2008. *Handbook of Critical and Indigenous Methodologies.* London: Sage.

Dwyer, Alexander. 2018. "Toward the Formation of Genuine Partnership Spaces." *International Journal of Students as Partners* 2 (1): 11-15. https://doi.org/10.15173/ijsap.v2i1.3503.

Enloe, Cynthia. 1996. "Margins, Silences and Bottom Rungs: How to Overcome the Underestimation of Power in the Study of International Relations." In *International Theory: Positivism and Beyond* edited by Steve Smith, Ken Booth, and Marysia Zalewski, 186-202. Cambridge: Cambridge University Press.

Enloe, Cynthia. 2004. *The Curious Feminist: Searching for Women in a New Age of Empire.* Berkeley: University of California Press.

Felten, Peter, Julianne Bagg, Michael Bumbry, Jennifer Hill, Karen Hornsby, Maria Pratt, and Saranne Weller. 2013. "A Call for Expanding Inclusive Student Engagement in SoTL." *Teaching and Learning Inquiry* 1 (2): 63-74. https://doi.org/10.20343/teachlearninqu.1.2.63.

Freire, Paulo. 2002. *Pedagogy of the Oppressed*, thirtieth anniversary ed. New York: Continuum International Publishing Group.

Giroux, Henry. 1997. *Pedagogy and the Politics of Hope: Theory, Culture, and School*. Boulder, CO: Westview Press.

Healey, Mick, Abbi Flint, and Kathy Harrington. 2014. *Engagement through Partnership: Students as Partners in Learning and Teaching in Higher Education*. York, UK: Higher Education Academy. https://www.advance-he.ac.uk/knowledge-hub/engagement-through-partnership-students-partners-learning-and-teaching-higher.

Healey, Mick, Abbi Flint, and Kathy Harrington. 2016. "Students as Partners: Reflections on a Conceptual Model." *Teaching and Learning Inquiry* 4 (2): 1-13. https://doi.org/10.20343/teachlearninqu.4.2.3.

Kehler, Angela, Roselynn Verwoord, and Heather Smith. 2017. "We Are the Process: Reflections on the Underestimation of Power in Students as Partners in Practice." *International Journal of Students as Partners* 1(1): 1-15. https://doi.org/10.15173/ijsap.v1i1.3176.

Matthews, Kelly E. 2017. "Five Propositions for Genuine Students as Partners Practice." *International Journal for Students as Partners 1 (2)*: 1-9. https://doi.org/10.15173/ijsap.v1i2.3315.

Mihans, Richard, Deborah Long, and Peter Felten. 2008. "Power and Expertise: Student-Faculty Collaboration in Course Design and the Scholarship of Teaching and Learning." *International Journal for the Scholarship of Teaching and Learning* 2 (2): 1-9. https://doi.org/10.20429/ijsotl.2008.020216.

Seale, Jane, Suanne Gibson, Joanna Haynes, and Alice Potter. 2015. "Power and Resistance: Reflections on the Rhetoric and Reality of Using Participatory Methods to Promote Student Voice and Engagement in Higher Education." *Journal of Further and Higher Education* 39 (4): 534-52. https://doi.org/10.1080/0309877X.2014.938264.

Shor, Ira. 1992. *Empowering Education: Critical Teaching for Social Change*. Chicago: University of Chicago Press.

Silvers, Hannah. 2016. Student response to "Translating Partnerships: How Faculty-Student Collaboration in Explorations of Teaching and Learning Can Transform Perceptions, Terms, and Selves." *Teaching and Learning Inquiry* 4 (2): 13-14. https://doi.org/10.20343/teachlearninqu.4.2.5.

Smith, Heather. 2017. "Unlearning: A Messy and Complex Journey with Canadian Foreign Policy." *International Journal* 72, no. 2 (June): 203-16. https://doi.org/10.1177/0020702017711702.

Sylvester, Christine. 2009. *Art/Museums: International Relations Where We Least Expect It*. London: Paradigm Publishers.

Truth and Reconciliation Commission of Canada. 2015. *Truth and Reconciliation Commission of Canada: Calls to Action*. http://nctr.ca/assets/reports/Calls_to_Action_English2.pdf.

Tuhiwai Smith, Linda. 1999. *Decolonizing Methodologies: Research and Indigenous Peoples*. London: Zed Books.

Van Dam, Lianne. 2016. Student response to "Students as Partners: Reflections on a Conceptual Model." *Teaching and Learning Inquiry* 4 (2): 12-13. https://doi.org/10.20343/teachlearninqu.4.2.3.

Weller, Saranne, Grete Domarkaite, Joseph Lam Chung Lam, and Lidya Metta. 2013. "Student-Faculty Co-Inquiry into Student Reading: Recognising SoTL as Pedagogic Practice." *International Journal for the Scholarship of Teaching and Learning* 7 (2): 1-16. https://doi.org/10.20429/ijsotl.2013.070209.

Zalewski, Marysia. 1996. "All These Theories Yet the Bodies Keep Piling Up: Theories, Theorists, and Theorising." In *International Theory: Positivism and Beyond*, edited by Steve Smith, Ken Booth, and Marysia Zalewski, 340-53. Cambridge: Cambridge University Press.

Zalewski, Marysia. 2006. "Distracted Reflections on the Production, Narration, and Refusal of Feminist Knowledge in International Relations." In *Feminist Methodologies for International Relations*, edited by Brooke Ackerly, Maria Stern, and Jacqui True, 42-61. Cambridge: Cambridge University Press.

CHAPTER 2

From Novelty to Norm

Moving Beyond Exclusion and the Double Justification Problem in Student-Faculty Partnerships

Sean Wilson
Graduate student
Duke University
United States

Julie Phillips
Attorney
U.S. Government
United States

Helen Meskhidze
Graduate student
University of California Irvine
United States

Claire Lockard
Doctoral candidate
Loyola University Chicago
United States

Peter Felten
Executive director
Center for Engaged Learning
Elon University
United States

Susannah McGowan
Assoc. director for curriculum design
Georgetown University
United States

Stephen Bloch-Schulman
Professor
Elon University
United States

The scholarship of teaching and learning (SoTL) aims to investigate student learning in a disciplinary, inter-disciplinary, and systematic way. Though SoTL practitioners are deeply interested in the experiences of students and invested in student learning, students themselves are rarely included as collaborators in SoTL projects (Mercer-Mapstone et al. 2017). Students, because they are so rarely included, are typically viewed as novelties when they are involved in SoTL. Our focus in this chapter is on the experiences of students who *have* been included—specifically, students who partner with faculty to conduct SoTL research—and yet remain outsiders to the work in significant ways. Our research team is composed of four such students and three faculty members who frequently partner with students. We will be speaking from and analyzing our own experiences in the context of the broader SoTL community.

We begin with two anecdotes, each written by the former undergraduate students on our research team who worked in two independent student-faculty partnerships. These anecdotes highlight the fact that though we (the students) were being included in SoTL research, we nonetheless experienced a kind of exclusion from the SoTL community predicated upon a presumed set of norms regarding who has the capability to engage in SoTL activities. Put differently, even when we were included in the SoTL conversation, we confronted exclusionary barriers.

We, as a research team, then analyze these experiences with frameworks offered by two scholars who study oppression, Iris Marion Young and Kristie Dotson. We characterize these experiences as instances of what Young calls "internal exclusion" (2000, 53) and critically examine the justificatory norms that prevented the students on our research team from becoming full members of the SoTL community. We find that students (and the faculty who partner with them) bear a *double burden of justification.* We are excepted to produce high quality scholarship that contributes to the ongoing needs of the discipline and the students who should be the beneficiaries of our collective knowledge of how to teach for the best learning—an expectation that everyone in the field faces—and the additional burden of continually justifying students' engagement in and with SoTL. We offer suggestions to the SoTL community in the concluding section, particularly to faculty members, on how to affirm students' presence in SoTL and how to treat student partners more justly.

Anecdote #1: Policing Student Voices

Claire A. Lockard, Helen Meskhidze, and Sean P. Wilson

We were student members of a research team investigating the under-representation of female-identified people in philosophy several years ago. Our research team noticed a dearth of qualitative methods in the literature, so we decided to use focus groups as a means of gathering data on female-identified undergraduates' experiences in philosophy (see Lockard et al. 2017). Our inclusion as undergraduate researchers presented interesting methodological and epistemological opportunities and challenges. For instance, we took the lead in developing, facilitating, and transcribing focus groups consisting of female-identified undergraduate students with varying degrees of experience in philosophy. Our research team anticipated that excluding faculty researchers from this phase of our research would encourage students to speak more candidly regarding their gendered experiences.

We encountered a memorable challenge while presenting our work at the 2014 International Society for the Scholarship of Teaching and Learning (ISSOTL) conference in Quebec City. Our student-faculty panel had just presented potential reasons for the underrepresentation of women in philosophy departments. The opening response in the question time, however, was neither a question nor a comment about the content of our presentation. Instead, the audience member offered a recommendation for the two female-identified undergraduate presenters to change our voices: to speak up, to use less vocal fry (i.e., to not drop our voices' pitch), and to speak more like our male undergraduate colleague on the panel. This audience member went on to remark that vocal fry is a fitting metaphor for the way women do not feel heard in philosophy. The commenter suggested that if only women spoke up, things would improve. To our disappointment, much of the discussion devolved into us explaining why it was not our voices that were the problem. We wondered: would this comment have been made if we had been female-identified faculty, rather than female-identified students? During the break after the session, the female-identified students on the panel reflected on our voices and the times in our lives when we had been told to keep quiet. This experience was our central memory of the conference long after we left Quebec City, overshadowing numerous positive experiences we also had at ISSOTL 2014. Despite how important sharing power was among the students and faculty on our research team and the positive outcomes engendered by working in a student/faculty team, we were met with repeated institutional and personal challenges throughout this two-year project because of our status as students.

Anecdote #2: Exercising Power in Research

Julie C. Phillips

Two other undergraduate students and I joined with three faculty to collaborate on a research project about the differing perspectives of students and faculty on teaching literature reviews in political science (Rouse et al. 2017). Our project consisted of student researchers conducting interviews with political science faculty and undergraduate students to determine how students and faculty approach the literature review process. The interviews illuminated as much about student-faculty interactions as about the literature review process. Specifically, my fellow student researchers and I found that when conducting interviews, the student-teacher hierarchy was ever-present. Both the student researchers and the faculty interviewees instinctively fell into traditional roles of "student" and "teacher," despite the research-based context.

One particular faculty interview stands out. The method of the project was a traditional Decoding the Disciplines interview (Middendorf and Pace 2004): the student interviewer asked questions about how the faculty member taught literature reviews and conducted literature reviews in their own research. Participants answered our questions in the vast majority of our interviews. But in this particular interview, we were unable to guide the conversation. The professor sidestepped every question we asked, either by answering the question he apparently wanted to be asked or refusing to answer at all. His refusals were polite, but were refusals nonetheless. This was especially evident when we asked him to map out his literature review process on a whiteboard, and he refused to even attempt to do so. To say this was infuriating is an understatement. How were we supposed to get anything out of the research if the professor would not cooperate?

This one interview seemed like an outlier at first. But as we began conducting our analysis of the collected data, we quickly realized that this interview was comparable to the other faculty interviews. This prompted us to wonder why we had not noticed that trend during the other interviews. Why was something so obvious in a paper transcript inconspicuous during the interviews themselves? My fellow student researchers and I discussed the trend and concluded that we were not seen as researchers. We were seen as students. Even though we intended to present ourselves as members of academia on the same level as the faculty, the power dynamics associated with the student-teacher relationship remained (Cook-Sather and Felten 2017). And in that frustrating interview, what had felt like the professor's apathy was more a mutual failure to engage with the new dynamic of researcher-interviewee.

We were proud to have the opportunity to present at the inaugural EuroSoTL Conference in Ireland in June 2015. Throughout the conference, we often found ourselves being approached because of our novelty as student presenters. All of our interactions with other conference attendees were positive. During the Q&A following our panel, the audience was engaged and wanted to learn more about both the research and our experiences as students conducting the research. While we were still viewed as students, I felt that we were also viewed as fellow academics, albeit with less experience. This perception stems from the questions we received, which focused on our perspective as researchers, not just as students.

Theoretical Perspectives on Exclusion and Justification

These anecdotes do not represent the full range of student experiences in SoTL, but they illustrate how significant challenges may persist within student-faculty SoTL partnerships. We (the chapter authors) will now analyze some of these ongoing challenges using the vocabulary and tools of two scholars who study oppression. We do not mean to draw direct comparisons between the oppressed populations discussed by these scholars and students as a social group. We do, however, find the tools developed from the study of oppressive social systems to be useful in understanding the experience of students in SoTL (and this usefulness might give us all pause).

Iris Marion Young, in *Inclusion and Democracy*, highlights two types of unjust decision-making practices: external and internal exclusion. External exclusion occurs when certain individuals or groups are completely left out of decision-making, while others dominate and control it (Young 2000, 52). This form of exclusion is typified by decisions made behind closed doors by an exclusive group that fails to (or chooses not to) adequately consider the concerns of those who are not part of the decision-making process. Even as the importance of students as partners is heralded (see, for example, Felten 2013; Cook-Sather, Bovill, and Felten 2014; Healey, Flint, and Harrington 2014; Werder, Pope-Ruark, and Verwoord 2016; Matthews 2017), students are rarely included in SoTL projects as researchers, despite the fact that students are so central to the goals of SoTL. And even when students partner with faculty on SoTL inquiries, faculty often determine the focus, goals, scope, and roles of the research before the partnership begins (Cook-Sather, Bovill, and Felten 2014).

The solution to external exclusion may seem obvious: simply bring in more students. But external exclusion is only part of the problem. The anecdotes above illustrate that the second type of exclusion Young discusses, internal exclusion, is also at play. Internal exclusion prevents people from having the "opportunity to influence the thinking of others, even when they have access to fora and procedures of decision-making" (Young 2000, 55). Internal exclusion, for example, occurs when a conversation privileges certain styles of communication that may be inaccessible to some (Young 2000, 53). Internal exclusion occurs in the case of SoTL when faculty members—even well-intentioned ones—unknowingly or unreflectively dismiss or patronize students who are conducting or presenting SoTL research, as our anecdotes demonstrate.

One way that internal exclusion operates in the case of student participation in SoTL is through the pervasive call to justify students' presence as researchers. The concept of the burden of justification was put forward by Kristie Dotson as a barrier to inclusion in the field of philosophy. Dotson posits that the concept of "real" philosophy, or philosophy that incorporates "commonly held, univocally relevant, historical precedents," creates a barrier to more diverse perspectives entering the field (Dotson 2012, 5). Instead of analyzing their arguments, critics force philosophers who fall outside the bounds of "real" philosophy to defend their work as legitimate philosophy. People from marginalized populations and people who utilize uncommon philosophic methods tend to be called to do this justificatory work more than others, and this, in Dotson's view, might be one reason why these people often leave philosophy.

The above anecdotes illustrate that SoTL places similar burdens of justification, both explicitly and implicitly, on students and the faculty with whom they partner. We are frequently explicitly asked to talk about the reasons for having student participation, the difficulties of student participation, and the knowledge gained and lost because of student participation. Students' presence in SoTL is itself seen as unusual and thus worth interrogating, sometimes at the expense of a focus on and respect for the SoTL research being done. While we do not find it universally problematic to discuss students' involvement in SoTL research, we do worry about the shift in focus from the research itself to one particular aspect of the methods and the potential for internal exclusion during such discussions.

All academic research requires some form of explicit justification and legitimation. We argue, however, that student-faculty partnerships are faced with an additional burden of justification. As such, student-faculty partnerships are faced with the problem of double justification.

The above anecdotes also illustrate an implicit burden of justification that influences SoTL research. In the second anecdote, for instance: although the student researchers had expertise in facilitating interviews and understood the disciplinary norms, their status as students prevented faculty interviewees from fully engaging in the interviews. One reading of this is that perhaps faculty interviewees assumed because the student interviewers had not justified their presence as *researchers*, the students did not have the expertise needed to make any credible knowledge claims. The implicit call to justify their presence prevented students from fully occupying their roles as researchers.

Students in SoTL are diverse practitioners who are susceptible to exclusion, whether external or internal. To make the SoTL community more welcoming to diverse practitioners (in this case, students), we encourage SoTL to move away from asking "How can SoTL benefit from student participation?" or "How can SoTL benefit students as researchers/scholars?" to "How can SoTL practitioners make SoTL more welcoming to student researchers?" We borrow the framing of this question from Anita Allen, an African-American female-identifying philosopher, when she suggests that philosophers should "shift the burden to the discipline to explain why it is good enough for us; we should be tired of always having to explain how and prove that we are good enough for the discipline" (quoted in Dotson 2012, 4).

Toward a More Affirming SoTL

We contend that faculty must take responsibility for addressing the forms of exclusion already present and likely to persist within SoTL and students as partners work. SoTL-active faculty and staff cannot assume that this exclusion, especially internal exclusion, will be remedied by patiently waiting for more students to join the SoTL community, eventually tipping the cultural scales without any affirmative efforts by faculty and staff. Nor can faculty and staff ethically expect students to (continue to) justify their own presence within the SoTL community. As the powerful insiders of SoTL, faculty and staff must act.

But where to start?

Echoing Jenny Marie, who builds on Mick Healey's work, the community should ask *every* SoTL project, "Where are the students?" (2018, 39). A good first step is to recognize that we can only do the best research possible with student partners. The goal for perspectives toward student engagement is what Carmen Maria Marcous refers to as "affirmation." Marcous (2014) argued that affirmation requires the community both acknowledge that underrepresentation is a problem and prioritize efforts to address said problem. The SoTL community must recognize that student underrepresentation is problematic for the methodology and epistemology of the field.

Adopting the perspective that *we can only do the best research possible with student partners* shifts the burden of justification from inclusion to exclusion: it does not make the inclusion of students necessary but makes their exclusion automatically suspect and in need of justification. By systematically asking "where are the students?", we will prompt significant changes in SoTL practices—the processes we use to develop and value the questions that guide our inquiries, the research methods we employ to gather and analyze evidence, and the ways we present and write about this work.

As the student experiences detailed in this paper illustrate, however, growing students' presence will not necessarily be sufficient to address the chronic internal exclusion students encounter in SoTL or engender an attitude of affirmation throughout the community. Faculty and staff need to critically examine our own assumptions and privileges. When do we act in ways that exclude student partners or that cue the culture of justification in SoTL? In our enthusiasm for welcoming students into the SoTL community, are we unintentionally reinforcing exclusive practices and beliefs? Below we offer some suggestions and questions that arise from our own experiences as students and faculty in SoTL partnerships.

Because a central practice of the SoTL community is the presentation of research at conferences, interaction with students at conferences can be just as important as interaction with students while conducting the research. For participants in SoTL who are unfamiliar with working with students as researchers and peers, engaging with a student presenter may seem different from engaging with a faculty presenter. We thus suggest:

1. ***Before asking a student researcher a question, ask yourself: Would I ask a faculty researcher this question?***

    Student researchers are often the recipients of different types of questions than faculty researchers, as demonstrated in our anecdotes. We have argued that the difference in questions stems primarily from students being viewed as novelties in SoTL. Students are not treated as researchers because audiences want to learn more about their experiences as students. But if the students have not thematized their research position as students, such questions are often problematic. If, however, a presentation thematizes the students *as being* students, then questions about the student researchers as students are relevant.

2. ***Assume the value of students and students' perspectives.***

It is very often the case that students, and particularly undergraduate students, have less academic experience than professors. This lack of academic experience does not mean that students lack insight or understanding regarding their own research. We urge faculty to take student research just as seriously as they take their own or that of their faculty colleagues.

3. ***Make sure students are treated with respect and act as allies toward them.***

Faculty and staff need to hold respecting students as an imperative in formulating questions and comments for student researchers (Schroer 2007). For example, commenting on a student presenter's voice, as seen in the first anecdote, is not respectful. Nor is patronizing students, which can result from seeing students as outsiders. Faculty may need to call on one another to increase their respect and regard for students' voices in SoTL to ensure students are treated with respect. Active ally-ship is central for the kind of respect we envision and is an important element in ensuring that students will continue to bring valuable contributions to SoTL.

These steps demonstrate what should exist at the core of any partnership, particularly when partnerships go public.

Reflection Questions for Readers

Taking "How can SoTL practitioners make SoTL more welcoming to student researchers?" as our main question, we suggest our readers consider the following sub-questions:

- **For students**: Can you think of a time when you were taken seriously as a researcher? What happened to allow your inclusion, and how might that situation be replicated?
- **For faculty:** Can you think of a time when students were, from your perspective, taken seriously as experts and researchers? What

happened to allow their inclusion, and how might that situation be replicated?

- **For students:** What are some ways that student SoTL researchers can encourage one another either at conferences or during the research process? What are some ways that faculty and staff SoTL researchers have encouraged you?
- **For faculty:** What resources does your institution have to help you improve your collaborative practices in your SoTL research? What resources might you help develop further?

What Does the "Partnership" in Student-Faculty Partnerships Mean?
A Ruminating Postscript
Stephen Bloch-Schulman

In the editing phase of bringing "From Novelty to Norm" into print, an important issue was raised to the author team by the editors, Lucy Mercer-Mapstone and Sophia Abbot. Lucy writes on behalf of herself and Sophia:

> One point I would like to invite you to consider is what your structure and use of voice within certain sections communicate to the reader. I raise this because I think the way your wonderfully powerful messages are communicated may not be having the desired effect, or at least not one you intend. bell hooks discusses how, often when faculty invite student reflection with good intentions, they implicitly reinforce power hierarchies by asking students to share so much of themselves and their experiences in ways that faculty do not—thus placing students in a place of vulnerability while they remain "safe" in not having to do so. Something of that notion comes across to me (and to Sophia) in the way your piece is currently written: where students share vulnerable and uncomfortable experiences under their own names, while faculty partners do not, remaining anonymous in the use of the academic "we." I do

not think that it was your intent, but I think it important to consider that it may be construed that way. An additional connotation of that is that the "we" (faculty) appear to be examining the experiences of students, which is the antithesis of the powerful argument you make for authentic inclusion of students in SoTL. I don't doubt that you all constructed this piece together, but that doesn't come through explicitly.

Here, I would like to think on this comment both in light of the writing of "From Novelty to Norm" and to place the issues raised into a larger context of questions about equity in student-faculty partnerships. These issues are quite complicated and hard, if not impossible, to resolve in a short postscript or in the writing of any one chapter. My modest goal here is to highlight the complexities of the issues raised by Lucy and Sophia's concerns and to spell out how some of these were addressed or failed to be addressed by our process and in our chapter. Finally, I describe the way language around equality and equity point in the right direction but remain open to multiple interpretations. I advocate for those of us who engage in and write about these kinds of partnerships to think more carefully about what these terms might mean and why we highlight certain meanings over others. I end with a call for further discussion, hoping to center these conceptual questions when students and faculty engage in projects together.

The larger ethical and political challenges implied within the above comment, as I read it, is to ask what makes a partnership a partnership. Lucy and Sophia note hooks' suggestion that it is vulnerability that is *a* or *the* key to something deeper and more meaningful. And it is true, as the editors highlight, that the students' voices—and their ways of being emotionally and reputationally vulnerable—are the focus of the chapter "From Novelty to Norm." And faculty do not speak in the chapter from first-hand, personal experience. We faculty thus do seem invulnerable or hidden (or both) in this particular respect. An excellent point.

This point is all the more important because of how faculty typically write and show up in their work. Even as faculty turn up and are heard typically (though, of course, less for faculty from certain groups and of certain identities—a difference the importance of which is never to be underestimated), academic writing remains decontextualized, and authors (and, in SoTL, the subjects of our research) often remain generalized and disembodied. We often write as "the author" or "we," without any sense of who the author is, or who the collective "we" are. *[Note: this was true in the article as we originally wrote it, though, through editing, the authors hope that it is less present now than in earlier drafts.]* This points to a bigger and deeper set of questions about the nature of academic writing and the stance of authors and researchers—one well beyond the scope of this reflection, but one hinted at herein and needing more exploration, as Lucy and Sophia suggest.

So, faculty might be heard but heard in only certain, invulnerable—or maybe inhuman—ways (for more on this, see Cook-Sather, Abbot, and Felten, 2019). And students might be often generalized into "the students," rather than naming specific ones and noting their individual contributions.

It is, however, true that part of our hope is simply to raise the voices of the students so they are centered, given how—as the former-students eloquently speak to in this chapter—their voices are so often ignored. We faculty and administrative and academic staff are less likely to be ignored, so there is less need to highlight our voices (again, this is more true of those, like me, who are cisgender, white, straight men). This dynamic is often evident in the citation and acknowledgment practices within SoTL, where students are very rarely mentioned by name, even when they have contributed excellent ideas (being seen as "subjects" of the research and thus needing special protections), and faculty are often named and thanked (being seen as contributors). This is a difference especially important within academia, given that name-recognition and the connection between one's name and one's ideas are the coins of the realm. That is, there is a way, by working with students so their voices are heard, that faculty—who could publish elsewhere and be recognized for our own work—are sharing respect and risk. There is signal boosting here, along with a chance for faculty to encourage our own reflection and even self-criticism.

Another important note is that while Lucy and Sophia have rightly pointed to the way the first-hand experience and emotional work is uneven, there is another way we were quite intentional in attending to the historical and contemporary challenges for equity in student-faculty partnerships. Namely, in the typical way these projects place students in a position to speak personally while faculty do the heavy theoretical lifting. I have grown wary of the "students bring experience, faculty bring disciplinary expertise" model I often see in faculty-student collaborations. To avoid this, our authorship team explicitly shared the theoretical work. Claire (one of the student partners) did the heaviest lifting in reading, addressing, and making relevant the work of Kristie Dotson, whose writing is the most theoretically complex of the resources we used. I worked on and wrote the section about Iris Marion Young, which is more straightforward. So, in one way, her doing the theory-work made things more even. But even as we avoided the students-bring-experience/faculty-bring-theory dynamic, questions about equity persisted. Claire doing this theory-work may have been a form of exploiting her exceptional skills, when she has a dissertation to write and she had already put in significant effort on another section in the chapter, and I could have done the work (though likely not as well).

In my work on and thinking about student-faculty partnerships and questions of equity elsewhere, I have often turned to Iris Marion Young's political conception of equality in the workplace (Bloch-Schulman and castor 2015; Jacquart et al. 2019). Iris Marion Young (1990) argues that businesses embody forms of injustice by placing the "task-defining" work—that work of determining the goals and agenda of an organization and determining the main ways that organization will meet those goals—in the hands of the (often societally privileged) few, while leaving the "task-executing" work—the activities to achieve these goals—in the hands of the many. I have come to see that I want to help students develop these "task-defining" skills. Teaching students to set appropriate goals for their and the class's learning and to set the agenda allows them to gain invaluable experience.

It is not clear to me that we achieved this type of equity, either, though there were plenty of times when we agreed to split up the work and everyone had a chance to take on a challenge they were willing to or interested in. The current postscript is an example of having taken on this work—I volunteered to address the particular comment cited at the beginning of the chapter. This too has complicated matters; Lucy and Sophia asked me to expand the original postscript, making it long and my voice overrepresented relative to the overall length of the chapter.

Cook-Sather, Bovill, and Felten (2014, 4) define the principles of partnership as respect, reciprocity, and shared responsibility. They wisely note throughout their book that they are

> not suggesting that students and faculty get and give exactly the same things in pedagogical partnerships. Indeed, partnerships invite faculty and students to share different experiences and perspectives; those differences are part of what can make partnerships so rich and diverse.

But we might note, with our experience here and through the lens of Lucy and Sophia's comments, that what respect means for each of us might be quite different, as does the question of what *kind* of respect we are valuing.

Under various constraints, we might have to choose to highlight some goals in partnership over others. Figuring out which to value and when requires some reflection and leads to difficult choices that we should be explicitly discussing within our partnerships and in our writing. Different equity focuses in partnerships address different educative and research goals, and—given how unlikely it is that we can address and achieve them all—we need to think carefully about which foci would help achieve the desired goals. For example, vulnerability might create deeper emotional connections between faculty and students and be a way for students to fully experience faculty as human beings who struggle, fail, and work hard in light of those struggles. But it wouldn't teach task-defining. Taking task-defining as a central goal of a partnership would allow students to play roles, both within groups and for themselves, of organizing and prioritizing. But teaching task-defining may be separate from, and not address, the kind of emotional vulnerability Lucy and Sophia call for and want to make more equal.

The questions raised here require judgment, and there are multiple problems to try to resolve at the same time: might Lucy and Sophia's suggestion for such equity in such a short chapter be another form of the double justification needed in this work? We typically don't expect vulnerability or equity in other academic products. Might there be other forms of equity that are more valuable in this particular context? Might there be solutions that are efficient and clear that we are missing, and could or should have been implemented?

I, therefore, invite you, reader, into some of my own uncertainty and ask you to join me in addressing these multiple and complex questions—with Lucy and Sophia (now part of the conversation, too).

Reflection Questions for Readers

Thinking on the discussion of equity in this chapter's postscript, consider:

- What are the possible separate educative goals for different people in student-faculty partnerships?
- How should we, and who should, decide which of these goals we should value and strive for?

References

Bloch-Schulman, Stephen, and maggie castor. 2015. "I Am Not Trying to Be Defiant, I Am Trying to Be Your Partner: How to Help Students Navigate Educational Institutions that Do Not Value Democratic Practice." *Partnerships: A Journal of Service-Learning & Civic Engagement* 6, no. 1 (Winter): 161-80. http://libjournal.uncg.edu/prt/article/view/1099/749.

Cook-Sather, Alison, Sophia Abbot, and Peter Felten. 2019. "Legitimating Reflective Writing in SoTL: 'Dysfunctional Illusions of Rigor' Revisited." *Teaching & Learning Inquiry* 7 (2): 14-27. https://doi.org/10.20343/teachlearninqu.7.2.2.

Cook-Sather, Alison, Catherine Bovill, and Peter Felten. 2014. *Engaging Students as Partners in Learning and Teaching: A Guide for Faculty*. San Francisco, CA: Jossey-Bass.

Cook-Sather, Alison, and Peter Felten. 2017. "Ethics of Academic Leadership: Guiding Learning and Teaching." In *Cosmopolitan Perspectives on Academic Leadership in Higher Education*, edited by Feng Su and Margaret Wood, 175-91. London: Bloomsbury Academic.

Dotson, Kristie. 2012. "How Is this Paper Philosophy?" *Comparative Philosophy* 3 (1): 3-29. https://doi.org/10.31979/2151-6014(2012).030105.

Felten, Peter. 2013. "Principles of Good Practice in SoTL." *Teaching & Learning Inquiry* 1 (1): 121-25. https://doi.org/10.20343/teachlearninqu.1.1.121.

Healey, Mick, Abbi Flint, and Kathy Harrington. 2014. *Engagement through Partnership: Students as Partners in Learning and Teaching in Higher Education*. York, UK: Higher Education Academy. https://www.advance-he.ac.uk/knowledge-hub/engagement-through-partnership-students-partners-learning-and-teaching-higher.

Jacquart, Melissa, Rebecca Scott, Kevin Hermberg, and Stephen Bloch-Schulman. 2019. "Diversity is Not Enough: The Importance of Inclusive Pedagogy." *Teaching Philosophy* 42, no. 2 (June): 107-39. https://doi.org/10.5840/teachphil2019417102.

Lockard, Claire, Helen Meskhidze, Sean Wilson, Nim Batchelor, Ann J. Cahill, and Stephen Bloch-Schulman. 2017. "Using Focus Groups to Explore the Underrepresentation of Female-Identified Undergraduate Students in Philosophy." *Feminist Philosophy Quarterly* 3 (4). https://doi.org/10.5206/fpq/2017.4.4.

Marcous, Carmen Maria. 2014. "How to Solve the Diversity Problem." *APA Newsletter on Feminism and Philosophy* 13, no. 2 (Spring): 22-27. https://cdn.ymaws.com/www.apaonline.org/resource/collection/D03EBDAB-82D7-4B28-B897-C050FDC1ACB4/FeminismV13n2.pdf.

Marie, Jenny. 2018. "The Relationship Between Research-Based Education and Student-Staff Partnership." In *Shaping Higher Education with Students: Ways to Connect Research and Teaching*, edited by Vincent

C. H. Tong, Alex Standen, and Mina Sotiriou, 30-40. London: UCL Press.

Matthews, Kelly E. 2017. "Five Propositions for Genuine Students as Partners Practice." *International Journal for Students as Partners* 1 (2):1-9. https://doi.org/10.15173/ijsap.v1i2.3315.

Mercer-Mapstone, Lucy, Sam Lucie Dvorakova, Kelly E. Matthews, Sophia Abbot, Breagh Cheng, Peter Felten, Kris Knorr, Elizabeth Marquis, Rafaella Shammas, and Kelly Swaim. 2017. "A Systematic Literature Review of Students as Partners in Higher Education." *International Journal for Students as Partners* 1 (1):1-23. https://doi.org/10.15173/ijsap.v1i1.3119.

Middendorf, Joan, and David Pace. 2004. "Decoding the Disciplines: A Model for Helping Students Learn Disciplinary Ways of Thinking." *New Directions in Teaching & Learning* 98 (Summer): 1-12. https://doi.org/10.1002/tl.142.

Rouse, Mary, Julie C. Phillips, Rachel Mehaffey, Susannah McGowan, and Peter Felten. 2017. "Decoding and Disclosure in Students-as-Partners Research: A Case Study of the Political Science Literature Review." *International Journal for Students as Partners* 1 (1). https://doi.org/10.15173/ijsap.v1i1.3061.

Schroer, Jeanine Weekes. 2007. "Fighting Imperviousness with Vulnerability: Teaching in a Climate of Conservatism." *Teaching Philosophy* 30, no. 2 (June): 185-200. https://doi.org/10.5840/teachphil200730225.

Werder, Carmen, Rebecca Pope-Ruark, and Roselynn Verwoord. 2016. "Students as Co-Inquirers." *Teaching & Learning Inquiry* 4 (2): 1-3. https://doi.org/10.20343/teachlearninqu.4.2.2.

Young, Iris Marion. 2000. *Inclusion and Democracy*. New York: Oxford University Press.

Young, Iris Marion. 1990. *Justice and the Politics of Difference*. Princeton, NJ: Princeton University Press.

CHAPTER 3

Unlearning Hierarchies and Striving for Relational Diversity

A Feminist Manifesto for Student-Staff Partnerships

Rachel Guitman
Undergraduate student
McMaster University
Canada

Anita Acai
PhD candidate
McMaster University
Canada

Lucy Mercer-Mapstone
Lecturer
University of Sydney
Australia

We are three women who have been thinking and practicing in the partnership space for several years. At the time of writing this chapter, we were also students: two postgraduate and one undergraduate. We hail from opposite sides of the globe: Australia and Canada. We bring a deep complexity of identity to this space, which we want to acknowledge and celebrate with our use of the collective "we." Drawing on this complexity, we have something to say.

We are writing this manifesto and stepping out of the "safe space" of traditional scholarly writing. We are removing the caveats, the footnotes, the sections on limitations. Scholarly articles on higher education pedagogy and practice often require acknowledgments that bound, contextualize, warn against, and childproof what authors really want to say. Perhaps that is apt in our risk-averse environment. Here, though, we do not seek safety. We step into those "brave spaces" (Arao and Clemens 2013, 135) that require honesty and vulnerability. We share with you our hopes, fears, and aspirations for partnership.

This manifesto was deeply informed by the words and ideas of bell hooks and Chandra Mohanty. These two influential feminists and education activists have been with us in thought and spirit as we have developed as scholars and as humans. Drawing on their words, we argue the need for two important changes within academic institutions. The first is to acknowledge, critique, and re-conceptualize traditional power asymmetries through a process of "**unlearning hierarchy.**" The second is to broaden conceptions of academic relationships in a shift toward "**relational diversity.**" We propose the field and practice of partnership is a catalyst, source, and site for these changes.

Partnership: What's in a Name?

Scholars use many names when writing about collaborative and equitable relationships focused on matters of teaching and learning in higher education. Our space of expertise is probably most familiar to you as "students as partners" or "student-staff partnership" (which includes faculty in the North American context). As we have done thus far, however, we choose to call this "partnership," explicitly focusing on the equitable relationship rather than on labeling the groups partaking in it. Partnership need not only be between students and staff. As this manifesto demonstrates, students can also partner with other students to make their voices heard. Thus, we seek to use the term "partnership" in the most inclusive sense.

Pedagogical partnerships can occur in many contexts, including learning, teaching, and assessment; subject-based research and inquiry; scholarship of teaching and learning; and curriculum design and pedagogic consultancy (Healey, Flint, and Harrington 2014). Drawing on its ethos as an aspirational and values-based practice, Cook-Sather (2016, 2) has argued that partnerships can create "counter-spaces" that challenge hegemonic discourses. It is on this aspect of partnership—power—that we focus in this manifesto. Partnerships in higher education allow us to aspire toward more equitable institutions—institutions where existing power structures and patriarchal norms are challenged.

Toward Change: Unlearning Hierarchies and Striving for Relational Diversity

In her efforts to unsettle patriarchal, racially inequitable systems at her institution, bell hooks writes that she found that "almost everyone, especially the old guard, were more disturbed by the overt recognition of the role our political perspectives play in shaping pedagogy than by their passive acceptance of ways of teaching and learning that reflect biases" (hooks 1994, 37). What change demands of us, then, is an overt effort to counteract the implicit norms that are broadly and passively accepted in institutions.

Such change brings significant resistance and discomfort because it inherently requires the unseating of traditional power-holders. In discussing the espoused rhetoric of institutional shifts toward cultural diversity, hooks describes an unsettling scene:

> Many of our colleagues were initially reluctant participants in this change. Many folks found that as they tried to respect "cultural diversity" they had to confront the limitations of their training and knowledge, as well as a possible loss of "authority." Indeed, exposing certain truths and biases in the classroom often created chaos and confusion. The idea that the classroom should always be a "safe," harmonious place was challenged. (1994, 32)

Does this sound familiar to you? For us, this tension reminds us of many discussions with staff about sharing responsibility for teaching and learning with their students. This was particularly apparent for us within our positions as students speaking to those in positions of power. Perhaps, then, what we are experiencing in this trend toward partnership is akin to the movement for cultural diversity, but instead, we are pushing for a new type of "**relational diversity**" in our universities. And just as hooks talks about individuals needing to "unlearn racism" in moving toward cultural diversity, we need to urge ourselves, our colleagues, and our institutions to create spaces in which we can "**unlearn hierarchies**."

In early discussions about this manifesto, we referred to the notion of "unlearning power" as opposed to "unlearning hierarchies." We later rethought this idea. Some partnership work describes partnership as a space where we can overcome or transcend power. We don't believe this is possible given that power will always exist as an inherent aspect of social organization. As a (perhaps imperfect) metaphor, we instead liken power to energy: the first law of thermodynamics states that energy can be neither created nor destroyed but only transferred or transformed from one form to another. Power, in the same way, is rarely overcome or ceases to exist. To suggest power can be overcome or erased, or for that to be an aim, ignores structures and histories that have shaped current systems and practices, and risks advocating empty, meaningless forms of diversity. This suggestion silences rather than opens up conversations about critically engaging with issues of power. Chandra Mohanty, for instance, writes:

> The central issue, then, is not one of merely *acknowledging* difference; rather the more difficult question concerns the kind of difference that is acknowledged and engaged. Difference seen as benign variation (diversity), for instance, rather than as conflict . . . or the threat of disruption, bypasses power as well as history to suggest a harmonious, empty pluralism. (1989, 181)

Although hierarchical ways of working will likely not cease to exist in institutions, we envision an institutional sphere that has room for more diverse forms of relationships, where predefined roles are not the only options. The goal then is to create *space* for relational diversity: for heterogeneity, variation, and self-determination in relationships within institutions. Rather than try to unlearn power, we need partnership practices and scholarship that acknowledge and critique existing power structures—practices that aspire toward social change which, as with energy, dynamically transfer and share power throughout the relationship. In a hierarchical setup, power is concentrated at the top; if partnership is genuinely embraced as a mode of functioning, however, it can move us in the direction of sharing power more equitably among different institutional stakeholders. Partnership can drive such change by offering a counter-space for individuals to critically examine and redistribute power, sharing voice and centrality among those who may previously have been silent and marginalized. As students, for example, we have encountered multiple, empowering partnerships where our expertise and leadership were recognized and valued. This has been liberating. Part of this value comes from the fact that partnerships present a way of working that is in stark contrast to the hierarchies we routinely come up against in other areas of the academy.

Mohanty, in her work, discusses the example of race, arguing for a "fundamental reconceptualization of our categories of analysis so that differences can be historically specified and understood as part of larger political processes and systems" (1989, 181). Indeed, marginalized groups must be explicitly centered when unlearning hierarchies situated in this historical and systemic context. We thus call for scholarly ways of working that overtly seek to not only include but center epistemologies, experiences, and knowledges of historically marginalized groups. Partnerships have the potential to accomplish this when members of and scholarship by historically marginalized groups are core to their projects.

Unlearning hierarchies is no small feat, but in this manifesto, we have chosen to be aspirational, setting agendas for future action. Partnership as a movement challenges classic, hierarchical notions of staff as experts and students as receptacles for knowledge. Such spaces allow for the recognition that partners do not necessarily contribute to partnership in the same ways; yet, each contribution brings something unique and should be equally welcomed, valued, and respected (Bovill, Cook-Sather, and Felten 2011). This applies equally to student or staff status and to other axes of social identity such as gender, race, class, or (dis)ability.

In this effort, we are reminded by Peter McLaren that the goal of this movement is not to eliminate conflict and challenge but rather to embrace it as part of necessary criticality:

> Diversity that . . . constitutes itself as a harmonious ensemble of benign cultural spheres is a conservative and liberal model of multiculturalism that, in my mind, deserves to be jettisoned because, when we try to make culture an undisturbed space of harmony and agreement where social relations exist within cultural forms of uninterrupted accords we subscribe to a form of social amnesia in which we forget that all knowledge is forged in histories that are played out in the field of social antagonisms. (Quoted in Steinberg 1992, 399)

As we operate in a political moment that seems averse to healthy conflict, we feel it is important to note that our call for relational diversity is not a call for an "undisturbed space of harmony and agreement." Similarly, to Mohanty's insistence on a historical, power-involved grounding for change, we must openly embrace the struggle, difficulties, and contradictions involved in employing partnership within institutions. The importance of constructive conflict in partnership is increasingly being acknowledged (Abbot and Cook-Sather, under review; Mercer-Mapstone et al. 2017). It would not be helpful, for example, to enact partnership with the underlying assumption that students and staff are in equal positions when staff traditionally have held (and do hold) more power in institutions. We must face past and present hierarchies head-on, honestly, and with our eyes wide open. Otherwise, we risk arriving at an endpoint of the kind of false multiculturalism McLaren describes—one where we forget the inherent and necessary struggle towards equity, born from "social antagonisms" grounded in unequal power relations.

Beware of Neoliberal Seduction

If we continue to look to feminist thought for insight, we are reminded of a cautionary tale. We can draw a parallel between the commodification of gender and the ways in which students are frequently commodified in higher education. Each of these examples shows how the kind of inequalities we seek to redress are actually sustained. For example, constructing gender as a binary has put a greater focus on the things that make women different from men, thereby allowing for the commodification of femininity. A case in point is the production of items targeted at girls and women, which actively produce and police standards of femininity.

Similarly, focusing on the distinction between students and staff often creates situations in which students are commodified. The label of "student" can mean more grant funding for a project or initiative, a ticked inclusivity box, or improved institutional performance indicators. We have each experienced such situations. It serves the system well to perpetuate the distinction between students and staff. That distinction allows universities to market themselves more attractively to the consumer: students.

In seeking change, we must be aware that we do so in a climate of commodification and consider how such an environment risks negating our efforts. For example, actions that break down barriers and remove labels threaten those in power who stand to benefit from differentiation, but the rhetoric of leveling hierarchy benefits universities because it fits the current zeitgeist. Here again, we see powerful resonance with feminist action, which has been commodified in efforts to make it unthreatening. An example is major corporations that maintain male-dominated power structures and working environments while producing ads with strong women to profit off of our desire for social change without actually changing. In partnership, too, there is the risk of its adoption in lip service only: buying into the neoliberal seduction of institutional rhetoric to curry favor with student "clients," without the authentic enactment of partnership (Bell and Peseta 2016). In such cases, students act merely as figureheads and not as true partners. As women and as student partnership practitioners, we have felt this kind of commodification both in relation to our gender and our involvement in partnership, and thus caution against it.

Collective Agency

Intentional partnership can be an act of resistance against the consumerist model of neoliberal higher education which reinforces the passivity (rather than agency) of students (as written about more extensively by colleagues such as Bryson 2016). We have previously written about such spaces as "sites of resistance" against patriarchal power (Acai,

Mercer-Mapstone, and Guitman, 2019). We have personally felt the potential of these spaces and relationships in empowering us as women and as students. The process of writing this manifesto, for example, has given each of us a deep sense of comradery and empowerment. Following our Skype meetings, as we close our browsers from opposite hemispheres and rise up from our chairs, we do so with a sense of vibrating energy. Hyped up on the excitement of subversive ideas and collective pushback against the powers-that-be, we take this energy into our own respective worlds where it flows into all aspects of our lives and across our networks. When it comes to building effective resistance, it is vital to seek out and connect such spaces for collective action. As Mohanty reminds us:

> Resistance lies in self-conscious engagement with dominant, normative discourses and representations and in the active creation of oppositional analytic and cultural spaces. Resistance that is random and isolated is clearly not as effective as that which is mobilized through systemic politicized practices of teaching and learning. Uncovering and reclaiming subjugated knowledge is one way to lay claims to alternative histories. But these knowledges need to be understood and defined pedagogically, as questions of strategy and practices as well as of scholarship, in order to transform educational institutions radically. (1989, 185)

If striving for relational diversity in universities through partnership is an act of resistance against power hegemonies, then it is not enough for those sites of resistance to be happening in isolation. Rather, as Mohanty insists, we need to work with collective agency as activists and advocates—systematically and politically—if we are to see the kind of change toward which we aspire. To ensure that change remains authentic, we must also be open to partnership in its many forms. We must bear in mind that it is values and behaviors that define a partnership, and not where it comes from or how it is labeled (Matthews 2017; Mercer-Mapstone and Mercer 2017).

Nothing we have mentioned here is easy or comfortable! But if we follow hooks' lead and look to previous movements for social change—for example, civil rights and feminist liberation—we learn that:

> To create a culturally diverse academy we must commit ourselves fully. . . . We must accept the protracted nature of our struggle and be willing to remain both patient and vigilant. To commit ourselves to the work of transforming the academy . . . we must embrace struggle and sacrifice. We cannot easily be discouraged. We cannot despair where there is conflict. Our solidarity must be affirmed by the shared belief in a spirit of intellectual openness that celebrates diversity, welcomes dissent, and rejoices in the collective dedication to truth. (hooks 1994, 33)

The "we" of which hooks talks here must be conceptualized in the broadest sense. In the same way that feminism is not just a "women's issue," it is critical that those already within the partnership community increasingly look outward. It is important that the current "we" reach out and extend the boundaries of our practices, our discussions, and our networks to welcome newcomers with an ethos of absolute inclusivity. Knowing the kinds of considerate, open, and radical people in the partnership community, we have faith that it is within our capacity to engage in such an effort. As interest in and enactment of partnership grows in the academy, it is important to remember the lessons we can learn from feminist theorists. Together, as a community, we can work to unlearn hierarchy and broaden relational diversity in our own institutions and beyond.

Reflection Questions for Readers

- What practices have you found to contribute to the more equitable distribution of power in higher education relationships? How might these practices contribute to enhancing relational diversity in your context?
- Do you have relationships which give you nourishment? How might you grow or develop those to support relational diversity?

- What emotions does the notion of "unlearning hierarchy" evoke for you, and why?
- What first steps could you take to ensure that power dynamics and histories are critically examined in your new or existing partnerships?

References

Abbot, Sophia, and Alison Cook-Sather. Under review, 2019. "The Productive Potential of Pedagogical Disagreements: From Conflict to Clarity in Classroom-Focused Student-Staff Partnerships." Unpublished, last modified May 22, 2019.

Acai, Anita, Lucy Mercer-Mapstone, and Rachel Guitman. 2019. "Mind the (Gender) Gap: Engaging Students as Partners to Promote Gender Equity in Higher Education." *Teaching in Higher Education.* https://doi.org/10.1080/13562517.2019.1696296.

Arao, Brian, and Kristi Clemens. 2013. "From Safe Spaces to Brave Spaces: A New Way to Frame Dialogue Around Diversity and Social Justice." In *The Art of Effective Facilitation: Reflections from Social Justice Educators*, edited by Lisa M. Landreman, 135-50. Sterling, VA: Stylus Publishing.

Bell, Amani, and Tai Peseta. 2016. "Students as Partners—A Way to Re-Shape Higher Education Pedagogy or Neoliberal Seduction?" Paper presented at the Higher Education Research and Development Society of Australasia Conference, Fremantle Australia, July 2016. https://theycallmedrbell.com/2016/10/05/students-as-partners-a-way-to-re-shape-higher-education-pedagogy-or-neoliberal-seduction/.

Bovill, Catherine, Alison Cook-Sather, and Peter Felten. 2011. "Students as Co-Creators of Teaching Approaches, Course Design, and Curricula: Implications for Academic Developers." *International Journal for Academic Development* 16 (2): 133-45. https://doi.org/10.1080/1360144X.2011.568690.

Bryson, Colin. 2016. "Engagement Through Partnership: Students as Partners in Learning and Teaching in Higher Education." *International Journal for Academic Development* 21 (1): 84-86. https://doi.org/10.1080/1360144X.2016.1124966.

Cook-Sather, Alison. 2016. "Creating Brave Spaces Within and Through Student-Faculty Pedagogical Partnerships." *Teaching and Learning Together in Higher Education* 18: 1-6. https://repository.brynmawr.edu/tlthe/vol1/iss18/1/.

Healey, Mick, Abbi Flint, and Kathy Harrington. 2014. *Engagement through Partnership: Students as Partners in Learning and Teaching in Higher Education.* York, UK: Higher Education Academy. https://www.advance-he.ac.uk/knowledge-hub/engagement-through-partnership-students-partners-learning-and-teaching-higher.

hooks, bell. 1994. *Teaching to Transgress: Education as the Practice of Freedom.* New York: Routledge.

Matthews, Kelly E. 2017. "Five Propositions for Genuine Students as Partners Practice." *International Journal for Students as Partners* 1 (2): 1-9. https://doi.org/10.15173/ijsap.v1i2.3315.

Mercer-Mapstone, Lucy, Sam Lucie Dvorakova, Lauren J. Groenendijk, and Kelly E. Matthews. 2017. "Idealism, Conflict, Leadership, and Labels: Reflections on Co-Facilitation as Partnership Practice." *Teaching and Learning Together in Higher Education* 21: 1-9. https://repository.brynmawr.edu/tlthe/vol1/iss21/8/.

Mercer-Mapstone, Lucy, and Gina Mercer. 2017. "A Dialogue Between Partnership and Feminism: Deconstructing Power and Exclusion in Higher Education." *Teaching in Higher Education* 23 (1): 1-7. https://doi.org/10.1080/13562517.2017.1391198.

Mohanty, Chandra T. 1989. "On Race and Voice: Challenges for Liberal Education in the 1990s." *Cultural Critique* 14: 179-208. https://doi.org/10.2307/1354297.

Steinberg, Shirley R. 1992. "Critical Multiculturalism and Democratic Schooling: An Interview with Peter McLaren and Joe Kincheloe." *International Journal of Educational Reform* 1 (4): 392-405. https://doi.org/10.1177/105678799200100407.

CHAPTER 4

Power, Partnership, and Representation

A Dialogue Exploring Student Academic Representation Systems as a Form of Partnership

Abbi Flint
Educational developer and researcher
United Kingdom

Hannah Goddard
Student engagement consultant
The Student Engagement Partnership
United Kingdom

In this chapter, we draw on research which explored the role, value, and impact of student representation ("rep") systems (Flint, Goddard, and Russell 2017). This qualitative study involved interviews with senior staff in six higher education (HE) providers (universities/colleges), staff responsible for rep systems in their associated students' unions, and four national experts. We felt it important to include both provider and students' union (SU) perspectives as representation is an area where staff and students, HE providers and SUs, work collaboratively toward a common goal of high-quality academic experiences for students. Through this research, key themes emerged around relationships (including partnerships) and power in relation to rep systems, and it is the intersection between these that we explore in this chapter.

Some of the terms we use may be unfamiliar to those working and studying outside the United Kingdom (UK) or may have multiple meanings, so we have contributed terms to the online glossary for the book. Since rep systems are so central to our chapter, we define the term here: Student academic representation systems are a model of student involvement in the governance of universities; they are structured systems in which individual (elected or selected) student representatives (reps) speak and act on behalf of their (collective) peers concerning the educational and scholarly experiences of students (Flint, Goddard, and Russell 2017). We encourage you to consult the online glossary for an extended definition of rep systems, as well as explanation of other terms used throughout the chapter.

We've written this piece as a dialogue as it enabled us to explore the complexity of this area of practice in a discursive and thought-provoking way. We draw on Bohm's (1996) framing of dialogue as a means of developing and deepening shared understandings by building on one another's ideas and insights. Given that dialogue is often recognized as a key feature of partnership, this approach also models partnership in practice. The questions we use as prompts are informed by our research themes and are listed below:

- How do we understand power in representation systems?
- What can we learn by looking at representation systems through the lens of partnership?
- How might partnership in rep systems differ to other staff-student partnerships?
- What impact does effective partnership have on concepts of student power in rep systems?
- How might rep systems negotiate between individual and collective student partnership, and what are the challenges here?

The Dialogue
How do we understand power in representation systems?

Hannah: There's something to unpick in how we frame power in rep systems, and that's the balance between *power* and *empowerment*. Rep systems often exist within predetermined provider structures, with student voice and feedback expected within those spaces. For example, rep systems are usually aligned to the committee structures of the provider. This creates tension in our understanding of power; do these systems only have power with permission? On the other hand, UK rep systems are usually positioned as having a degree of independence from the provider (see Grills 2015), and while this is vital, it's worth reflecting on whether the current structures are set up to facilitate and enable that independence in the most successful way. Independence enables effective representation, accountability, and credibility, all of which were mentioned in our research as being highly important.

Abbi: I think that the issue of independence is really interesting. I'm reminded of Chapman, Blatchford, and Hughes' (2013) description of SUs and providers being *inter*dependent, and the challenges in maintaining a balance between holding the provider accountable and working together on issues of joint concern.

Hannah: I'd also mention that, in our research, representation was almost universally felt to achieve positive change, but how this manifested depended on how the values of representation were framed, and how much power is afforded to the system. I'm reminded of two contrasting quotes from participants:

> We need to be very careful: [student representatives] are not our reps. And that is difficult to explain to people, they're not our reps, they're student reps. [. . .] But, as soon as we let them speak, they may not say what we want but that's ok because that's what their role is. (Provider participant quoted in Flint, Goddard, and Russell 2017, 27)

> The students who attend those meetings, they don't hold any of the power. [. . .] If we are invited to a university meeting, on quality processes, it's inaccessible to most university staff let alone students. [. . .] We can't really say that there's equal power. It's not a joint birthday party if somebody else has organised it all and invited all their mates, but you get to go. (Students' Union participant quoted in Flint, Goddard, and Russell 2017, 28)

The workings of power and who holds it are very different in these two examples. I think a lot of this comes down to the ways different rep systems are positioned, and how they understand the value of student voice.

Abbi: To me, these quotes speak to a clash between the desire for partnership and the realities of the existing mechanisms through which partnership is expected to operate. In the first quote, a provider participant describes the importance of foregrounding the independence and autonomy of student reps. In the second, an SU participant describes how this is constrained by the largely provider-owned and -controlled spaces where representation operates. The image of the not-really-joint birthday party contrasts sharply with another provider participant's metaphor of reps as "architects of their experiences," which formed the title of our report. The term "architects" suggests a significant level of control, design, and ownership.

Hannah: I'd echo a point made by one of our participants: that a bit of power has to be relinquished by the provider for positive, effective change to be led by students. I believe that when this happens, we see the truest examples of partnership working and where reps are given space to be those architects.

Abbi: Yes, it's important to recognize that it may be hard for student reps to claim this power themselves when they operate within provider-owned or -led structures and processes. One of our SU participants approached this by being a "wedding crasher": inviting themselves to meetings to get a seat at the table.

Hannah: Absolutely. There are many complexities at work when we start unpicking what power means in and for student voice and representation. For me, this is where having a clear vision and set of values becomes essential. This enables you to access power, whether through self-empowerment or through that access being agreed at the outset, for example, through that seat at the table. The challenge is that effective rep systems often entail a bit of both—power within structures and power that the reps assert for themselves.

Abbi: I wonder if there is potential to move beyond oppositional understandings of power and shift to think about "power with" as Taylor and Robinson (2009) suggest. In previous work, Mark O'Hara and I reflected on links between community and power for student reps (Flint and O'Hara 2013). Part of feeling a sense of belonging is having influence within your community (McMillan and Chavis 1986). *Would reframing rep systems as a joint community of staff and students help to work toward ideas of shared power and influence?*

What can we learn by looking at rep systems through the lens of partnership?

Abbi: I was interested that some participants aspired to partnership framings of rep systems. To me, this indicated that they could see the practical and conceptual potential of looking at rep systems in this way. One of the most exciting things about partnership is its transformative potential (Healey, Flint, and Harrington 2014). If we use partnership as a lens to explore how different parties work together it might help us to challenge assumptions we have of one another, question the roles we play, and reflect on whether the approaches we use constrain or enable effective ways of working (and learning) together. In this way, partnership can open up new ways of working within rep systems.

Hannah: This reminds me of a comment from a provider participant in our research, who emphasized that for any institution to be successful, it must put students at the heart of what they do. For me, a working partnership model would reflect this ethos and be led by it. Concerning representation specifically, if a provider/SU has a partnership framing, then this should inform and shape every aspect of how representation operates within that context.

As we discussed earlier, there's a values-based relationship between partnership working and independent, authentic student voice; if the shared goal is ensuring that students have positive experiences, then rep systems can play a "critical friend" role as a part of the partnership undertaking. A mature partnership doesn't mean only operating with consensus—partners can and should hold each other to account.

Abbi: I wonder if part of this complexity lies in the fact that rep systems are described in multiple ways: as simultaneously being a mechanism for student voice, consultation, *and* partnership. This is tricky, as consultation and partnership are different forms of student engagement. The approaches and relationships we build to enable consultation may not be effective in fostering partnerships. It might be worth asking ourselves— *what would a rep system look like if it was designed with staff-student partnership as an underpinning principle? How might current structures and processes be changed to build partnership relationships and ways of working?*

Hannah: Absolutely. A partnership framing necessitates thinking again about how power is operating within the provider context. Ideally, this would be collaborative with students and staff talking openly about what needs to change for students to feel empowered, and how they can shape this, addressing questions such as whether to use formal meetings or not, who sets the agenda for the meeting, who drives it, who delivers actions, and so on. A critical question in reflecting on how partnership could be embedded is: *what "space" can be made by the provider and the SU for the empowerment of student representatives?*

Abbi: Yes, and I think where partnership offers a different lens on this is that it goes beyond empowering one party; partnership encourages us to look at the active participation of both parties, how they share power, and their roles and responsibilities. This can be a developmental and empowering experience for staff as well as student partners.

Hannah: I'd like to expand a bit here on how the language used in the UK can sometimes be at odds with a partnership approach. Changes in the HE sector have largely been informed by a framing of education as a commodity, with higher education being described as a market and the student/staff or student/institutional relationships being transactional. For me, this is encapsulated in the fact that "higher education provider" is now a set phrase in the UK. But what does that mean, to be "a provider"? I don't think that students are "receivers" of education, and neither do many staff working in HE, so there's this tension between a consumer mindset and a resistance to it that has to be considered. A partnership approach challenges this latent consumerism. The focus isn't on a transaction but is instead about different stakeholders collaborating in meaningful ways.

How might partnership in rep systems differ to other staff-student partnerships?

Abbi: The UK literature makes a distinction between two aspects of student engagement: how students invest their time and energy in their own learning and research; and student involvement in institutional governance and enhancement. As a form of student engagement, the nature and purposes of partnership in these areas will be different. Partnerships in rep systems may be more like collegial relationships to enhance learning and teaching institutionally, whereas in the classroom staff-student partnerships may focus more on individual learning. In our research, participants recognized that while rep systems led to benefits for individual representatives, they also led to benefits for the provider, the SU, and the wider student body. I think it's also interesting to reflect on where partnerships in representation happen, often outside of formal learner-teacher relationships. I'm thinking here of Cook-Sather and Alter's (2011) discussion of liminality in partnerships, and *whether student representatives could be considered to be in liminal or hybrid roles?*

Hannah: The framing of purpose within rep systems and other partnership or engagement projects is significantly different, as well as the partnerships themselves that we're talking about. For representation within a UK context, it's not just a partnership between the representatives and localized staff—this partnership often extends up to informal or formal partnership agreements or commitments between the provider and the SU at a strategic level. This means that, as with a lot of the elements of a successful rep system, we see operation across a range of levels and contexts with partnership existing between students and academics, students and students, students and professional staff, students and the SU, the SU and the provider, and so on.

The partnership we see within representation is often embedded and longitudinal; it outlasts the experiences of each cohort of representatives and even of individual staff. It's a value system, and therefore helps to inform partnership planning at a strategic and project level. Having that investment and accountability means that rep systems can deliver strong partnership, and that partnership delivers strong rep systems.

Abbi: I think it's also worth reflecting on where enhancement-focused staff-student partnerships emerge beyond rep systems, for example in the scholarship of teaching and learning and projects to enhance the student experience. Some of our participants included these kinds of activities in their definitions of academic representation, and others saw them as complementary to it. For some, there was a sense that these other initiatives afforded flexibility and different ways of working that their formal rep systems did not. *What can we learn from informal/ extra-curricular partnerships to inform how rep systems work as part of a wider ecosystem of partnership?*

What impact does effective partnership have on concepts of student power in rep systems?

Abbi: This question speaks to why I first became involved in work around student engagement and partnership. As an educational developer, I was working around cultural change in learning and teaching using participatory approaches, and it seemed natural to me that, as students are part of the university community, they should be part of that change process. One of the purposes of rep systems is to influence and effect changes that enhance student learning experiences. If we are interested in engaging student reps and SUs in that process of change, then I think we should acknowledge and support students' agency in that process.

Hannah: The National Union of Students (2012) positioned democratic representation at the core of partnership, but our research and the conversations we have across the sector show this playing out in very different ways. Some students see partnership as positive for power, others say without partnership they don't have power, and others see partnership as a loss of independent power.

Abbi: That's fascinating, as I think that partnership and agency go hand-in-hand: partnership is recognized as being fostered through sharing power and responsibility. As Arnstein (1969, 216) noted, "Participation without redistribution of power is an empty and frustrating process for the powerless." A rep system rooted in partnership should support the agency of both staff and student partners.

Hannah: So, successful partnership working means reframing power, but this shouldn't be thought of as a loss. Necessitating a greater sharing of power requires openness, trust, and accountability, and that to me is something you gain by working in this way.

How might rep systems negotiate between individual and collective student partnership, and what are the challenges here?

Hannah: This distinction is very important for effective representation, and it is often where the system gets tangled. It's worth spending some time on this, as a common question asked by staff is: "how representative of students' views are the comments made by reps?" (see Little et al. 2009). While this question can be useful, there's also a risk of it undermining the effectiveness of representation.

Abbi: Why do you think that is?

Hannah: Because representatives and representative structures are often navigating between two distinct roles that aren't considered very often—that of acting as a "voice for" students or presenting the "voice of" students (Lizzio and Wilson 2009; Carey 2013). To summarize, "voice for" relates to the collective role of a representative, and "voice of" reflects the individual voice of that representative as a student. Rep systems by design are pluralistic, with multiple roles, values, and expectations being juggled by and between representatives and stakeholders, often without a clear articulation of what is required and when it will be required. *Is the representative in the meeting expected to speak on the basis of unfiltered* *consultation, or from their individual perspective of what it means to be a student on that course at that particular provider?*

The ways we navigate this in the rep system might also offer lessons to partnership more broadly because this same tension exists. The challenge and strength of effective representation is balancing individual and collective voices. This is expected of providers across the UK as the revised Quality Code for Higher Education (Quality Assurance Agency 2018) specifically mentions "actively engag[ing] students, individually and collectively, in the quality of their educational experience." I'd, therefore, emphasize that individual and collective partnership should operate at every level within and outside of representation.

Abbi: There is a strong vein in scholarship around partnership that speaks to relational models of engagement; in many cases, this is framed as individual relationships between students and staff. Many of our research participants emphasized the importance of individual relationships between key provider and SU staff, and those that worked in partnership had built strong professional relationships. While a focus on building trust and respect through these relationships is clearly important to successful partnerships, it's both challenging and fascinating to think about how this might work at scale and translate to collective relationships, such as those between student cohorts and teaching teams, or institutional leadership and SUs. There's potential here to open up the scholarship of student engagement and partnership to explore how we can learn from collective relationships in other fields. *Is this an area where SUs could contribute to the study of partnerships?*

Where Can We Go from Here?

We've tried throughout this dialogue to draw out some of the questions and intersections from our research themes. We're particularly interested in how understandings of partnership and of power shape the role, value, and impact of rep systems, and vice versa, as considerations of these often-tricky areas deliver stronger rep systems and therefore stronger student voice. In thinking about how you might develop student-staff partnerships in institutional governance and enhancement, we invite you to revisit the questions in italics posed throughout this dialogue. In addition, we've provided some questions below which are informed by the recommendations from our research, and by the conversations we've had since its completion.

Reflection Questions for Readers

Questions on partnership

- How are students' experiences, expertise, and ideas currently represented in your context? How might you use the ideas in this chapter to move toward working through empowered partnership within representation systems or similar student engagement practices?
- What opportunities are available within your context for active and collaborative partnership working? How is this informed by, or posing challenges to, existing concepts of power?

Questions on power

- How can you assess/redress the power relationships operating within your partnerships? This could include reflecting on visible signs of power such as: Who chairs meetings? Who sets the agenda? How are decisions made? How much authority is given to student voice?
- What purposes are you expecting your partnerships to fulfill? To what extent do current operational aspects facilitate or inhibit the achievement of these purposes?
- If you were designing a representation system from scratch, with partnership as an underpinning principle, what would it look like?

References

Arnstein, Sherry. 1969. "A Ladder of Citizen Participation." *Journal of the American Institute of Planners* 35, no. 4 (July): 216-24. https://doi.org/10.1080/01944366908977225.

Bohm, David. 1996. *On Dialogue*. London: Routledge.

Carey, Philip. 2013. "Representation and Student Engagement in Higher Education: A Reflection on the Views and Experiences of Course Representatives." *Journal of Further and Higher Education*, 37 (1): 71-88. https://doi.org/10.1080/0309877X.2011.644775.

Chapman, Paul, Sarah Blatchford, and Elgan Hughes. 2013. "Lightening Up the Dark Side: A Partnership Approach between a Students' Union and the University." In *Student Engagement: Identity, Motivation and Community* edited by Claus Nygaard, Stuart Brand, Paul Bartholomew, and Luke Millard, 271-90. Faringdon, UK: Libri Publishing.

Cook-Sather, Alison, and Zanny Alter. 2011. "What Is and What Can Be: How a Liminal Position Can Change Learning and Teaching in Higher Education." *Anthropology and Education Quarterly* 42, no. 1 (March): 37-53. https://doi.org/10.1111/j.1548-1492.2010.01109.x.

Flint, Abbi, Hannah Goddard, and Ellie Russell. 2017. *Architects of their Experience: The Role, Value and Impact of Student Academic Representation Systems in Higher Education in England*. London: The Student Engagement Partnership. http://tsep.org.uk/architects-of-their-experience-research-on-student-academic-representation-systems/.

Flint, Abbi, and Mark O'Hara. 2013. "Communities of Practice and 'Student Voice': Engaging with Student Representatives at the Faculty Level." *Student Engagement and Experience Journal* 2 (1). http://dx.doi.org/10.7190/seej.v1i1.64.

Grills, Aidan. 2015. "The Relationship between Universities and Students' Unions." Association of Heads of University Administration. https://ahua.ac.uk/the-relationship-between-universities-and-students-unions.

Healey, Mick, Abbi Flint, and Kathy Harrington. 2014. *Engagement through Partnership: Students as Partners in Learning and Teaching in Higher Education*. York, UK: Higher Education Academy. https://www.advance-he.ac.uk/knowledge-hub/engagement-through-partnership-students-partners-learning-and-teaching-higher.

Little, Brenda, William Locke, Anna Scesa, and Ruth Williams. 2009. *Report to HEFCE on Student Engagement*. London: Centre for Higher Education Research and Information (CHERI). The Open University. http://oro.open.ac.uk/15281/1/Report_to_HEFCE_on_student_engagement.pdf.

Lizzio, Alf, and Keithia Wilson. 2009. "Student Participation in University Governance: The Role Conceptions and Sense of Efficacy of Student Representatives on Departmental Committees." *Studies in Higher Education*, 34 (1): 69-84. https://doi.org/10.1080/03075070802602000.

McMillan, David W., and David M. Chavis. 1986. "Sense of Community: A Definition and Theory." *Journal of Community Psychology* 14, no. 1 (January): 6-23. https://doi.org/10.1002/1520-6629(198601)14:1%3C6::AID-JCOP2290140103%3E3.0.CO;2-I.

National Union of Students. 2012. *A Manifesto for Partnership*. National Union of Students. https://www.nusconnect.org.uk/resources/a-manifesto-for-partnership.

Quality Assurance Agency. 2018. *The Revised UK Quality Code for Higher Education*. http://www.qaa.ac.uk/docs/qaa/quality-code/revised-uk-quality-code-for-higher-education.pdf.

Taylor, Carol, and Carol Robinson. 2009. "Student Voice: Theorising Power and Participation." *Pedagogy, Culture and Society* 17, no. 2 (June): 161-75. https://doi.org/10.1080/14681360902934392.

CHAPTER 5

Partnership as a Civic Process

Isabella Lenihan-Ikin
Undergraduate student
Victoria University of Wellington
Aotearoa New Zealand

Brad Olsen
Undergraduate student
Victoria University of Wellington
Aotearoa New Zealand

Kathryn A. Sutherland
Associate professor
Victoria University of Wellington
Aotearoa New Zealand

Emma Tennent
PhD student
Victoria University of Wellington
Aotearoa New Zealand

Marc Wilson
Professor
Victoria University of Wellington
Aotearoa New Zealand

In a challenge to the "students as consumers" discourse, a team of students and academics at Victoria University of Wellington in Aotearoa New Zealand set out to investigate and demonstrate the potential of partnership as a civic process in research and in teaching. We were thrust together as a group of (mostly) strangers through a Change Institute experience in May 2017. Despite all odds (not knowing each other, different disciplinary backgrounds, different ages and stages of life, and no experience with "students as partners"), we became a cohesive team who examined civic engagement initiatives in curricula at our university. We conducted interviews; we developed case studies, resources, and even a new staff-student partnership program for the wider university; and we made recommendations for encouraging change across the institution. In this chapter, we offer a poetic summary of our project's research findings, and we treat the university as a civic realm and community with its own intrinsic power dynamics. We reflect on how our project challenged, unravelled, and got caught up in those power relations. We offer some celebrations of and warnings about growing partnerships in curricula and in research.

What Does "Civic" Mean in New Zealand?

New Zealand universities have a legally mandated role to be the "critic and conscience of society" (Education Act 1989, 162.4). Our universities work "interactively in, with and for society" (Brown et al. 2016, 648). Universities raise awareness about social issues, advise on and help create policy, conduct and share research that influences decision-making bodies and changes lives, and help students develop their ability to become (more) educated, engaged, and active citizens (see Wood and Mulligan 2016) and critical members of society. Universities are proponents for, partners in, and sites of civic engagement.

Many conceptions of civic engagement position "the university" as outside, critiquing, and/or working alongside "the community" (see Marullo and Edwards 2000). At one extreme, these asymmetrical relationships are based on a novice-to-expert paradigm, while others are more equal partnerships with reciprocal learning at their core (Brown et al. 2016). A capacious view of civic engagement also recognizes the civic identity of the university community itself. For example, Victoria University of Wellington is based in New Zealand's capital city and defines itself as a "global civic university" with the aim of "enriching national culture, civil society and global citizenship" clearly spelled out in our Strategic Plan (Victoria University of Wellington 2014). Many of our degrees, qualifications, courses, and extracurricular programs have been developed to help students and staff achieve this goal. Victoria is one of the city's largest employers, with more than 2,200 staff and over 22,000 students. An organization of this size is arguably a civic space in and of itself, as well as an organization that has a responsibility to speak truth to the power of the capital city and the nation (Boland 2014). We sought not only to investigate how best to encourage university-community partnerships through civically engaged curricula but also to challenge our own conceptions of and engagement with the university itself as a civic space.

Our Project

Our provost selected a team in early 2017 of two students and two academic staff members to attend a Students as Partners Change Institute at McMaster University in Canada. While the academics knew each other, and the students knew each other, we were essentially a team of strangers, jumping on a plane to cross the world and figure out some possibilities for extending our university's students as partners repertoire.

Our team sought to enact a partnership approach based on the Māori concept of *ako*, which means both to teach and to learn. We would all be learning from and teaching each other—in partnership. We laid out our expectations for partnership at our first meeting: it would be equitable, the administrative load would be shared, and we would recognize and draw on each other's strengths and expertise (once we knew what those were!). We committed to rotating tasks such as setting dates and chairing meetings, taking notes, identifying readings, and sharing the load of investigating flight and accommodation options. All this worked well before and during the Change Institute. But when we returned and the rubber hit the road in terms of getting our research project rolling, the partnership became somewhat less equal, though hopefully still equitable. We reflect on the challenges and thrills from that partnership later in this chapter. First, we briefly describe the project we undertook and some preliminary findings from our research on civically engaged curricula.

Victoria's 2017-2021 Learning & Teaching Strategy/Te Rautaki Maruako includes the aspirational goal that "all graduates will have the opportunity to participate in civic engagement and/or experiential learning" (10). Both civic engagement and experiential learning are described by Kuh (2008) as high-impact pedagogies that dramatically enhance student learning. Before implementing such practices on a wide scale, we aimed to celebrate what was already successful and learn from those engaged in such high-impact practices. Victoria staff who had demonstrated a commitment to embedding civic engagement in the curriculum were interviewed at micro (course), meso (program or Faculty), and macro (university) levels. With the help of a PhD student who joined our team as a research assistant, we conducted nine interviews: two pilots (to practice interviewing and test our questions); three with individual lecturers; three with six program/Faculty leaders; and one with a former senior leader. Our findings, shared below in poetic form, provide insights into the enablers and barriers for introducing and sustaining civically-engaged curricula. The poem is composed entirely from the words of our interviewees. All interviews are represented in the poem, which captures some of the key themes that came through in our research: voice and identity; outsiders and subversion; fear and risk-taking; and time and labour.

Embedding Civic Engagement in Curricula: Challenges, Joys, and Possibilities

A poem composed from the words of our research participants

Civically engaged curricula . . .
    treat the classroom as a civic space,
        bringing people in and sending
        students out into the broader community;

    recognize that the young people
        we have in our universities are themselves
        active citizens, with their own voices;

    ask of students,
        "What are your biases?
          How do you interact with your discipline?
            How do you interact with society?";
share what the students from last year's cohorts discovered;

    enable students to respond to real issues in a client organisation;

    encourage critique of power structures and ask,
        "Well, is this normal?

Should it be this way?
Why should it *not* be this way?"

If it's not pedagogically grounded
in students' learning, then it's just
volunteering.

Civically engaged lecturers . . .
take risks
It felt precarious
and like really carving out new territory,
so it had to be good because
it could be attacked
or undermined
or go terribly wrong;

encourage students to take risks
I'm not going to let students be
complacent or take things for granted,
students get shaken up;

manage risks
You're dealing with people's lives
and agendas
and the reputation of the university
and students' well-being;

build relationships
People encourage *me*
to experiment and
find my own voice and
my own way—and that's
what I encourage others to do.

Civically engaged universities . . .
show sympathetic leadership and
are positively disposed toward community involvement;

ensure the student body is itself diverse;

keep a handle on what's going on and
    don't exhaust the capacity of their collaborators;

develop policy AND support grassroots initiatives;

wedge open doors and show others the possibilities.

Civic engagement *thrives on goodwill,* and we fear that's not sustainable:
    Here's me on my hamster wheel chasing the cheese . . .
        I felt like I was flapping in the wind . . .
            I don't want to rock the boat.

 Civic engagement *welcomes naïve interventions* from outsiders:
    I was completely unaware of the system,
    which was a strength because
        if you knew about it, you'd
            never do it
                because it's just so terrifying.

Civic engagement *takes courage*:
    I really ruffled some people's feathers . . .
        worked in the edginess . . .
            took an alternative approach which is a bit controversial.

Civic engagement *needs adequate resourcing*:
    these initiatives require more investment than traditional courses . . .
    there was an assumption that
        a student would want to do this for free . . .
    either it's a flop and it stops,
        or it's a success and we scale it up, and we can then
            find funding sources we weren't able to find before.

Civic engagement does not need *to keep* everybody *happy*:
    the risk is that you end up with something which is
    the lowest common denominator.
Civic engagement does not need *institutional inertia*:
    we could grow a whole lot faster if it wasn't for

certain rules and restrictions;
we keep getting pushback.
Civic engagement does not need *cumbersome bureaucracy*:
not to "dis" on this university, but
it's a really different culture and
if it's too many forms to fill out,
I just don't deal well.
It's like turning around a battleship.

At the end of a course where we have
encouraged students to be curious citizens, it's not
just another crazy exercise.
Instead,
afterwards,
students are like

"Oh, actually maybe there's a little more to this world than I thought."

The poem outlines the challenges and opportunities for incorporating civic engagement into the curriculum. Now, we show how our partnership process mirrored some of the same themes.

Voice and Identity: "You're dealing with people's lives"

Any students as partners project exposes the tension between equality and equity. One key observation is that a partnership project does not have to ensure *equality* between student and staff partners: that is unachievable (students do not have offices to host meetings in, academics do; students do not always get paid, academics do; research is not always a requirement of undergraduate study, but it is required of academics). Students as partners processes can, however, be *equitable.* This requires deliberate recognition of voice, identity, power, and privilege by all parties. Academic partners are not solely responsible for this, although, given their resource privilege, it is important academics acknowledge and own this responsibility where necessary. To manage these issues, partnerships must ensure that the voices of all parties are recognized.

In our partnership, Brad, Emma, and Isabella, as students, reflected that not only did they have plenty of opportunities to speak, but they also felt heard and included in all decisions.

Our students as partners approach made space (unintentionally and then deliberately) for the naïve voice. As undergraduate students, Brad and Isabella had no experience with educational research methods and would ask questions such as whether deviating from the interview questions was possible, and how the ethics process worked. This naïveté, in turn, made Kathryn, Marc, and Emma question things they took for granted, both in terms of how academic institutions work, under the institutional hood where students may not get to look, for example, as well as under the metaphorical hood(ies) of the students.

Outsiders and Subversion: "If you knew about it beforehand, you'd never do it because it's just so terrifying"

We all felt like outsiders at different points in our project—not knowing each other to begin with, not knowing the literature, not having done interviews before, not being an academic, not being a student, not having been on the team from the beginning. As indicated above, the naïve voice of the "outsider" can raise probing questions and challenge what others may take for granted. One tension was around the delayed outcomes of the research project. Both Brad and Isabella are active members in undergraduate student politics and were keen to see the findings of the research disseminated or implemented in ways that would immediately benefit students. The project's extended timeline led us to question at times whether we were involved in research for the sake of output rather than transformation.

The students as partners process (much like the civic engagement initiatives of our participants) can work to subvert the normal way of operating within the university. Not only are students and academics separated by barriers of age, power, and role, but we are also isolated by different disciplines. Forming interdisciplinary connections is not always facilitated by institutional structures, nor is forming links between undergraduate students, postgraduate students, and academic staff from different Faculties. The subversive potential of bringing together people from different backgrounds and finding a way to honor their perspectives is an exciting element of students as partners work.

Our team had not worked together before, and none of us were experts in the area of civic engagement. While this posed challenges (such as the time burden of reading up on new concepts), we believe our naiveté (shared and individual) was a strength. Our experience never actually matched the "terror" implied in the poem and this section's subtitle, but there were challenges we did not foresee. Naiveté can be a strength when it frees you from expectations about how things *should* work. Our naiveté has meant we have been able to construct our own version of the students as partners model and learn and adapt along the way.

Fear and Risk-taking: "It felt precarious"

The student as partners process can be risky for all involved, but it also presents opportunities for challenging assumptions, both personal and collective. One challenge we collectively reflected on was differing assumptions about knowledge and experience. Kathryn noted, for example, that she made assumptions about the undergraduate students' knowledge based on their maturity: because they seemed older than their years, she assumed they knew more than their three years at university had taught them. Meanwhile, Brad and Isabella noted that, while it was nice to be asked for their opinion and invited to make decisions, without prior knowledge of how the research would unfold (let alone the theoretical and methodological underpinnings of the process), they were ill-equipped to even begin to answer. Kathryn assumed the role of keeping the project on track but feared that her leadership decisions could be construed as dictatorial and that she was compromising the partnership philosophy. As new territory for all of us, it was sometimes scary realizing how much we had to learn about each other and about the process.

Time and Labour: "Don't exhaust the capacity"

Embarking on projects between academics and students requires commitment and time—commodities in scarce supply for both parties. We often struggled to find time for the project among our other work—it was always a secondary consideration after our other engagements. Kathryn and Marc, as academics, had their regular teaching to attend to, alongside their usual, subject-specific research endeavors and service commitments. Brad, Emma, and Isabella had their own classes or research to undertake—for which they were paying—alongside a host of other activities including paid work and social or extracurricular activities. Our project became the task that would be pushed back first.

Compounding the fact that the project took longer to complete than anticipated was the lack of clarity regarding how work should be divided. A tension existed between us requiring guidelines and deadlines to be formulated, and the desire not to boss others around. Yet such deadlines and guidelines are a critical component of success—without these, no one is clear on the path forward or the future body of work involved. Others looking to embark on their own partnership adventures would be wise to consider the desirability of forming a team with motivated but busy individuals who have competing commitments, or remunerating individuals to devote their attention solely to the task. Although the popular adage opines, "If you want something done, give it to a busy person," balancing this against those who can do the project justice is also a critical factor.

Ako in Action

As our poem illustrates, opportunities abound for engagement within and across the university, and beyond. We are all too often isolated in silos of Schools and Faculties, undergraduates and postgraduates, staff and students. But one of the joys and possibilities of a students as partners approach is that it harnesses connections within the university and reveals the possibilities for transformative, critical, and civic engagement not just *beyond* the university but also *within*; it is an exciting counterpoint to institutional inertia. Students as partners offers a way to "walk the talk" of civic engagement by breaking down barriers across the university, fostering connection and community, and allowing collaborative endeavors. Our students as partners experience afforded us the opportunity to learn from *and* to teach each other, in a wonderful expression of *akoranga* and reciprocity. We have chosen, in the creation of a new partnership program for the university, not to use the terminology "students as partners" but instead to name our nascent program Ako in Action, to reflect the equal nature of the partnership. Students do not have to assume a new identity "as partners" to participate in our new program: everyone involved does, academic staff included. In the section below, we conclude our chapter by posing some questions for anyone considering embarking on such a partnership project.

Reflection Questions for Readers
- Collective reflections can be side-lined in a rush to get to the "real" business. How have you carved out time for reflection?
- Team leaders may struggle with the challenges of making decisions and the fear of railroading other team members. What might be the benefits and drawbacks of nominating a leader to manage group time?
- How will you tackle power dynamics?

References

Boland, Josephine. 2014. "Orientations to Civic Engagement: Insights into the Sustainability of a Challenging Pedagogy." *Studies in Higher Education* 39 (1): 180-95. https://doi.org/10.1080/03075079.2011.648177.

Brown, Kim, Kerry Shephard, David Warren, Gala Hesson, and Jean Fleming. 2016. "Using Phenomenography to Build an Understanding of How University People Conceptualise their Community-Engaged Activities." *Higher Education Research & Development*, 35 (4): 643-57. https://doi.org/10.1080/07294360.2015.1137880.

Kuh, George. 2008. *High-Impact Educational Practices: What They Are, Who Has Access to Them, and Why They Matter.* Washington: AAC&U.

Marullo, Sam, and Bob Edwards. 2000. "From Charity to Justice: The Potential of University-Community Collaboration for Social Change." *American Behavioral Scientist* 43, no. 5 (February): 895-912. https://doi.org/10.1177/00027640021955540.

New Zealand Government. 1989. Education Act, No. 80. http://www.legislation.govt.nz/act/public/1989/0080/latest/DLM183668.html.

Victoria University of Wellington. 2014. "Victoria University of Wellington Strategic Plan." https://www.victoria.ac.nz/documents/policy/strategies/strategic-plan.pdf.

Victoria University of Wellington. 2017."Learning and Teaching Strategy: Te Rautaki Maruako 2017-2012." https://www.victoria.ac.nz/documents/policy/strategies/learning-teaching-strategy.pdf.

Wood, Bronwyn, and Andrea Milligan. 2016. "Citizenship Education in New Zealand: Policy and Practice." *Policy Quarterly* 12, no. 3 (August): 65-73. https://doi.org/10.26686/pq.v12i3.4599.

SECTION TWO

INTERSECTIONS

Annotations on the Spaces in Between

Nancy Chick
Director of the Endeavor Foundation
Center for Faculty Development
Rollins College
United States

"Engaging in learner-teacher partnerships in hierarchical educational structures is messy work fundamentally about human relationships in a particular socio-cultural context."
—*Kelly Matthews (chapter 7)*

"We are interested in thinking about partnership as a radical, political practice."
—*Rachel Guitman and Elizabeth Marquis (chapter 9)*

As I read the four chapters in this section, my mind immediately called up Gloria Anzaldúa's *Borderlands / La Frontera* (1987), a tour de force of prose and poetry, autobiography, essay, theory, history, and song. It is one of the most influential texts of my formative academic years. I periodically return to my old copy, annotated with blue, yellow, pink, black, purple, and green inks, each of which marks the different inquiries that have brought me back. Reflecting on the following chapters drew me to all the inks.

". . . the complex and multiple lives students inhabit outside the university."
—Tai Peseta et al. (chapter 6)

"I was looking in from the outside. . . . And in those moments, I didn't feel like I was a student per se."
—Amani Bell, Stephanie Barahona, and Bonnie Stanway (chapter 8)

"A Chicana *tejana* lesbian-feminist poet and fiction writer" (as begins her biographical blurb), Anzaldúa reminds us—in the book, in the idea of the book, and in the self that lived the book—that our identities are never singular. In the section "*Si le preguntas a mi mamá, '¿Qué eres?'*" (If you ask my mother, "What are you?"), Anzaldúa answers,

> We call ourselves Mexican, referring to race and ancestry; *mestizo* when affirming both our Indian and Spanish (but we hardly ever own our Black ancestry); Chicano when referring to a politically aware people born and/or raised in the U.S.; *Raza* when referring to Chicanos; *tejanos* when we are Chicanos from Texas. (63)

This was "intersectionality" before Kimberlé Crenshaw (1991) coined the term that has become the *sine qua non* for who we understand ourselves to be in the twenty-first century.

"So, there were several different spaces in-between—between the various languages, between students and staff, between generations, between cultures, and between hierarchies."

"It's richer at the edge."

—Amani Bell, Stephanie Barahona, and Bonnie Stanway (chapter 8)

Anzaldúa's Borderlands is, among other things, "wherever two or more cultures edge each other" and "where the space between two individuals shrinks with intimacy" (iii).

Here, she tells us, race, culture, class, gender, nationality, language, and history mix, producing "hybrid progeny, a mutable, more malleable species with a rich gene pool" (77).

"This [partnership] mindset has enabled me to enjoy aspects of my life a lot more because I recognize what I bring to the table." —Tai Peseta et al. (chapter 6)

"The whole partnership thing . . . is messing with what we do in higher education. . . . How is your partnership messy?" —Kelly Matthews (chapter 7)

"There was the aspect of translation between students' and academics' worlds. . . . The language academics use does not invite students into that space. . . . 'What's a colloquium? That doesn't sound like somewhere that students are welcome to go.'" —Amani Bell, Stephanie Barahona, and Bonnie Stanway (chapter 8)

Here, Anzaldúa tells us, she writes from all of her identities by the "switching of 'codes,'" specifically "from English to Castillian Spanish to the North Mexican dialect to Tex-Mex to a sprinkling of Nahuatl to a mixture of all of these" (iv).

But the multilingual text is not simply a representation or celebration of this complex identity. It forces readers to do some work in order to understand, and to reconsider assumptions about, the sovereignty of our language.

Indeed, what *is* a colloquium?

"We've all been students. . . . So, it's talking about our past and future selves." —Amani Bell, Stephanie Barahona, and Bonnie Stanway (chapter 8)

Now in conversation with Anzaldúa and the authors in this section, I think she'd agree with Amani Bell that faculty and staff were once students. And arguably still are. On every page of *Borderlands* is evidence of the presence of the past. (Also on every page of *Borderlands* is the annotated evidence of the presence of my own past.) "My Chicana identity," she says, "is grounded in the Indian woman's history of resistance" (21). How are faculty and staff identities grounded in their histories of being a student? How does (or should) that fundamentally change this concept of *student-staff* or *faculty-student partnership*?

And I wonder what she would make of the expressions *learner-teacher* or *student-staff* or *student-faculty partnership*. She might say it sets up two distinct, dualistic, and thus hierarchical groups. She might remind us that in her Borderlands, in this space in-between, in place of the hyphen, is a "massive uprooting of dualistic thinking" (80).

"I will admit to having a very 'us and them' mindset about the divide between academics and students."
—*Tai Peseta et al. (chapter 6)*

"In this context, partnership can function as a means of pushing back and doing things differently . . . and offers a re-humanizing space. . . . I'm struck by the potential need for 'both/ and' understandings of partnership's political work."
—*Rachel Guitman and Elizabeth Marquis (chapter 9)*

"We emphasize how a 'partnership mindset' is emerging as a feature in students' accounts of their lives outside the academy."
—*Tai Peseta et al. (chapter 6)*

Here, Anzaldúa tells us, "dormant areas of consciousness are being activated, awakened" (iii), forming a "new consciousness" that creates "a new mythos—that is, a change in the way we perceive reality, the way we see ourselves, and the ways we behave" (80). One of the most enduring concepts from *Borderlands* is what she calls "The Mestiza Way": "She puts history through a sieve. . . . She surrenders all notions of safety, of the familiar. Deconstruct, construct" (82).

And now here, in this revolutionary work among students, staff, and faculty, say the authors in this section, a "partnership mindset" is being awakened. They put roles, power, and hierarchies through a sieve.

"The language of 'students as partners' . . . asks us to unlearn what we think we know."
—Kelly Matthews (chapter 7)

Unlearn, learn.

References

Anzaldúa, Gloria. 1987. *Borderlands / La Frontera.* San Francisco, CA: Aunt Lute Books.

Crenshaw, Kimberlé. 1991. "Mapping the Margins: Intersectionality, Identity Politics, and Violence against Women of Color." *Stanford Law Review 43*, no. 6 (July): 1241-99.

CHAPTER 6

A Partnership Mindset

Students as Partners in and Beyond the Academy

Tai Peseta
Senior lecturer
Western Sydney University
Australia

Jenny Pizzica
Senior lecturer
Western Sydney University
Australia

Ashley Beathe
21C student curriculum partner
Western Sydney University
Australia

Chinnu Jose
21C student curriculum partner
Western Sydney University
Australia

Racquel Lynch
Former 21C student partner
Western Sydney University
Australia

Marisse Manthos
21C student curriculum partner
Western Sydney University
Australia

Kathy Nguyen
Former 21C student partner
Western Sydney University
Australia

Hassan Raza
21C student curriculum partner
Western Sydney University
Australia

The Students as Partners (SAP) literature is flooded with case after case from around the world of students, staff, practices, and institutions being transformed by authentic encounters of pedagogical partnership. We read narratives of students genuinely astonished that staff seek out their perspectives and act on them in some way that improves the student experience (Peseta et al. 2016; Bell et al. 2017). We come to learn that staff are reenergized by the thoughtfulness students display about their learning and education more broadly, despite the circling of contested SAP understandings and agendas (Sabri 2011; Matthews et al. 2018). We understand that there are significant learning gains for students when they are engaged in partnership initiatives in ways that are consequential to their futures. Students engage with their studies differently—with more agency—and start to see themselves as part of the university community. In many ways, these are precisely the kinds of educational and developmental outcomes that advocates of SAP are interested in disseminating more widely, despite the suggestion that SAP is better conceived as an ethos rather than a set of outcomes (Healey, Flint, and Harrington 2014). Taken together, these insights add compelling nuance to the evidence base for not only continuing SAP initiatives but also for scaling up these schemes for richer and thicker impact.

While acknowledging the transformative possibilities in the "powerful SAP narrative," in this chapter, we aim to push the scholarly conversation in a slightly different direction. In many ways, the SAP curriculum initiative we describe here as part of our work together at Western Sydney University (hereafter, Western) is entirely of the routine kind described above: staff, students, and additional partners toiling together in ways where they teach each other their version of the university through the mechanism of curriculum-making and renewal. Collaborative decision-making and opportunities for challenge, co-creation, and reciprocity are all apparent in the SAP initiative that has brought us into partnership. In addition to much of the literature about student voice, agency, and partnership (Cook-Sather, Bovill, and Felten 2014; Matthews 2016; Dunne and Zandstra 2011), our approach is influenced by Williams's (2008) notion, "teach the university." For Williams (2008, 26) and us, "study of the university enjoins students to consider reflexively the ways and means of the world they are in, and what it does to and for them." This is one of our points of departure from other SAP initiatives (note: the other departure is that, at Western, partnership extends beyond students and staff). An important aspiration for our SAP scheme is that *the university as an idea and institution* (Barnett 2013, 2016) becomes an object of inquiry and curiosity for students. Yet our insular focus on the university points to a conundrum that appears to have been insufficiently attended to in the existing SAP literature: how do we trace the imprint of SAP schemes onto the complex and multiple lives students inhabit *outside* the university?

Our goal, through interrogating our own SAP curriculum initiative, is to follow how student partners themselves notice the effects of SAP among the workplaces, communities, and families within which they live and labor. We emphasize how a "partnership mindset" is emerging as a feature in students' accounts of their lives outside the academy.

The Western Sydney University Context: 21st Century Curriculum Project

Western, like many universities, has embarked on a program of strategic institution-wide curriculum renewal known as the 21st Century Curriculum project (hereafter, 21C). At the heart of 21C is the concept of "partnership pedagogy," oriented toward the challenges of the future of work and society (Barrie and Pizzica 2019). Our partnership pedagogy comprises four co-creation stages—co-design, co-development, co-delivery, and co-credentialing—and three values—interdisciplinarity, interdependence, and integrity (Pizzica 2018). The idea is that the design of a 21st century university curriculum (and education) can no longer be the province of universities alone. Amid the rush to consider the potentially disruptive implications (and opportunities) in the future of work (PWC 2014; FYA 2017), contemporary university curricula require partnerships of all kinds. At Western, 21C is encouraging partnerships with the Greater Western Sydney community, professional business associations, our university network partners, industry, commercial providers, edu-venture partners, our research institutes, and most importantly, our students. The 21C project has set in motion a variety of strategies and tactics to advance these educational ambitions. First, it funded several pilot projects intended for Schools within Western to scope more flexible curriculum structures and course architectures as well as identify opportunities for partnership pedagogy at scale. Second, 21C facilitated a series of future of work and society curriculum disruption forums intended to give staff, partners, and students a space to deliberate on the research about the future of work and its implications for curriculum. Third, 21C funded proposals that promised an innovative approach to the development of partnership pedagogy curriculum and supported that work through a series of Curriculum MakerSpaces. Finally, it offered a mechanism to acknowledge and recognize the labors of these staff via the Western Educational Fellowship Scheme. Our student curriculum partners have been intimately involved in each of these phases of 21C work—puzzling over the challenges of partnership, their roles and identities, the precise nature of their expertise, and their interactions with academics, and forming views about how our University is engaging them in this conversation. It is this suite of initiatives that form the backdrop to our reflections on the partnership mindset.

On Developing a Partnership Mindset

The idea of a partnership mindset emerged organically from our conversations in preparing for our 21C work together. The academics—Tai and Jenny—have been working with our student partners—Ashley, Kathy, Chinnu, Marisse, Hassan, and Racquel—to interrogate our experiences of what partnership looks like outside the university context and our curriculum conversations together. Specifically, the concept of "partnership mindset" emerged from a story Hassan told us in one of our sessions about how he was beginning to see himself less as an "employee" (in his weekend pharmacy job) and more as a partner who was invested in the success of the business. It struck us that this "outside the university" context was worth exploring together.

Hassan: It is through being a 21C student partner that I have cultivated the partnership mindset that I now actively apply on a day-to-day basis within and outside of being a student. By partnership mindset, I mean carrying with me the unapologetic mentality of looking to develop genuine partnerships with individuals I come across every day. This mindset has enabled me to enjoy aspects of my life a lot more because I recognize what I bring to the table. At the university, this might be in the way I work with other students on a group assessment task or with university staff to develop future curriculum. Outside the university, I have become a lot more confident in my weekend job at a local pharmacy in bringing my knowledge into my workplace environment. Rather than clocking on in the morning and being eager to leave in the afternoon, I try to engage with the environment and give active suggestions regarding enhancement. I recently listened in on a conversation (more like a rant) between the pharmacist and the manager about how they should be cautious about hiring additional students with no direct interest in pharmacy. While acknowledging that I was an exception among their pool of student employees, they stated that the others just "simply don't care." This struck me as surprising as there is nothing particularly extraordinary about me compared to the other students, except perhaps my role as a student partner. It is my view that this partnership mindset can work for a graduate no matter their field or the future they aspire to. A student will likely learn and appreciate their own value, and not settle for the slave-like "just do what you're told" environment of casual work that afflicts many students. My student partner role is a big part (if not the cause) of this mentality.

Ashley: Becoming a 21C student partner has opened my eyes to the power and possibilities of collaborative partnership. As an education student, I am naturally interested in the curriculum. However, it wasn't until I became a student partner that I could delve into the inner workings of higher education and my own University. For the first time, I've had the opportunity to engage in conversation with students, staff, academics, industry and community partners to see first-hand the benefit of true collaboration. The role has allowed me to enter into local, regional, and international conversations in ways that have not only benefited my current studies but have also influenced the way I approach my employment both in and out of the university. These curriculum co-creation conversations have taught me how to negotiate unfamiliar territory with academics and build networks within and outside the university, and I am beginning to hold my own in curriculum decision-making. I have sharpened how I listen. I am starting to appreciate more fully the depth of knowledge and experience that individuals bring with them to the co-creation table, and I feel my own creativity and confidence growing too. I believe I will apply this partnership mindset to any career path I choose. For now, I can see the distinct value it will add to my future teaching practice.

Chinnu: My goal when I started university was to get out as quick as I could with that all-important piece of paper. I wanted to be a criminal lawyer and that was it! Now my goal is to make the best of being a student and be open to partnerships and opportunities. No job title restricts me as long as I'm doing something meaningful and worthwhile. This drastic change of mindset is largely due to my role as a 21C student partner. By working in partnership with academics, I've gained valuable experiences that have empowered me to recognize that there is more to me and my role. No one is *just* a student or *just* an employee. Whether it's in my profession or life generally, everything has become influenced by a partnership mindset. In situations where I have needed to put my problem-solving skills to work, I focus on mutual respect and try to ensure that all parties benefit in some way. A partnership mindset has become a critical part of how I see my volunteer work at my local church youth group. I know that *being a student* is the expertise I bring to the table as a partner. Similarly, each person in my youth group has a unique skill set too, one that I had failed to fully appreciate before my student partner role. This partnership mindset has made me value the importance of my own unique perspective—an awareness that's both enriching and empowering.

Racquel: As a mature aged student—one who'd experienced university more than twenty-five years ago, had a career and family, and then decided to pursue my passion—I will admit to having a very "us and them" mindset about the divide between academics and students. Exposure to the very idea of partnership pedagogy and SAP was foreign to me. It was a learning curve for us during the first few months. I didn't feel the intimidation that my fellow SAPs would often verbalize when we started. What I felt was a need to "make" academics understand the value of my input as a *current* student. The experiences of participating in the program have, however, developed in me a partnership mindset. What does that look like for me? How has it translated into other areas of my life? I have already learned a lot over the years about working as a team, both at work and in my family life. I am in partnerships in many areas of my life. What I realized is that, when in an institutional setting, I still seemed to have a hierarchical mindset. I had a leader/follower, teacher/student way of seeing. Through the 21C project, I have come to see that my views, experiences, and opinions can and do sway those that are implementing educational innovations at the University. And I see the translation of a partnership mindset to my other roles as well. I am more able to work with my laboratory leaders so that my contribution is more meaningful. In my volunteer positions, I understand that my opinion, even when I am not in a position of power, is valuable. And I can be in a truer partnership with my family. I can see how the work we are doing aims to cultivate authentic and meaningful partnerships, and I see more clearly how I am contributing as a change-maker to nurture a partnership mindset throughout the University.

Marisse: Being a 21C student partner has been (and continues to be) an enriching experience. How? It is enriching because, in being a student partner, I no longer turn up to Uni to listen to the lecture, then go to the tutorial, and finally, head home with the same mindset. Instead, I arrive at Uni with thoughts like: *Why is my learning guided this way? I've seen that learning objective before, but I don't know what it means. Why do we have a student placement in the middle of the semester?* It's questions like these—the day-to-day ones—that underpin my experiences. But the SAP initiative begs the question: who is the "student" not only inside the university but outside? Listening to others in our everyday lives—to diverse experiences—adds something valuable not only to the perceptions we have of ourselves but also the people we are listening to. Since joining the SAP conversation, I have realized just how much I use the skills I have learned in everyday life. I currently work at a high school in the afternoons where I mentor students. A lot of my afternoon is listening to students—listening to their explanations of being stressed, their questions, their discussions, their insights. I thought "listening" was a sign that I wasn't talking enough, perhaps not doing my job well enough. I have realized that truly listening is exactly what I should be doing. I was a student at school once, just like the students I mentor, and I remember having to digest information (almost too much to swallow) throughout the school day. When I saw myself as equal to the students, rather than being the one to provide all the information, the students began driving their own learning and discussions. This is exactly how I feel by being in the SAP conversation. When I listen to these high school students, I discover the diversity in the room, and I recognize how different all these students are, which helps me to partner with them in meaningful and beneficial ways for all of us. Finally, I must return to this "enriching" idea of SAP—student partners will not only become better students at university, but they will also collect skills that are transferable into alternate settings outside of the university—skills that a lecture or tutorial cannot give you.

Kathy: As both a student and a university staff member, I often view my work and study as two separate parts of the same institution. I have held many casual jobs at the university, yet it is in my role as a 21C student partner where I am collaborating with academics and senior staff and contributing to effective student-staff relationships. I have gained more confidence in working in an organization with complex hierarchies. The experience has changed the way I communicate with others. It has helped me recognize the diversity of background and status of individuals in those conversations, and it has encouraged me to make those conversations productive. Perhaps it is my age and experience, but the chance to be a 21C student partner has been one of the most rewarding and impactful projects that I have been part of. I feel a sense of empowerment and pride in being at the forefront of representing student opinions and making change at the university, and this carries over into the other employee roles I have at the institution too. One of the best things I have taken away from the SAP experience is the sense of empowerment, pride, and confidence in all aspects of my life, but most notably in my work within the university, as it gives me a new outlook on my role within the sector.

Closing Reflection

We are only just beginning to notice and explore the emergence of a partnership mindset or disposition. Even in its nascent stages, the partnership mindset is there in the way we notice a more open engagement with colleagues and clients in our workplaces. It is there in the ways we value the difference and diversity people bring to conversations. It is there in how we are expanding from an "us/them" mentality between students and academics to one of genuine inquiry. It is there in the way we have started to recognize that we have a responsibility to use our agency wisely, no matter the context. And the partnership mindset is there in the way we carry ourselves in the world. These are substantial realizations that have, in many ways, been deeply profound.

The next step for our student curriculum partnership initiative at Western is to conceptualize how we become more mindful, inclusive, and design-focused on growing a partnership mindset in the way we communicate the rationale for our work and its likely effects on students' lives outside the university. This is an important narrative that can revitalize models of SAP so that it is more expansive than those which focus on power dynamics inside the university (important as that is) to include the idea of "partnership mindset," which gives universities yet another way of telling a story about its inherent social purpose. Perhaps most importantly, it is likely our students who are going to be the best advocates of working in partnership with others.

Reflection Questions for Readers

- What other examples of the "partnership mindset" beyond universities are in the SAP literature?
- How do we design SAP models and programs that help us to wrestle with, theorize about, and trace their impact outside our university communities?
- To what extent might narratives from employers/families/communities—i.e., those outside the university—help us to demonstrate the impact of SAP beyond the university? Is this an important argument for universities to be able to make empirically?

- If you have been involved in SAP, how have those experiences translated into aspects of your life outside of the university context? If you haven't been involved in SAP, what other learning from university do you see influencing your daily life in other contexts?

References

Barnett, Ronald. 2013. *Imagining the University*. New York: Routledge.

Barnett, Ronald. 2016. *Understanding the University.* New York: Routledge.

Barrie, Simon, and Jenny Pizzica. 2019. "Reimagining University Curriculum for a Disrupted Future of Work: Partnership Pedagogy." In *Education for Employability: Learning for Future Possibilities (Volume 2)*, edited by Joy Higgs, Will Lets, and Geoffrey Crisp, 143-52. Rotterdam, The Netherlands: Sense-Brill Publishers.

Bell, Amani, Tai Peseta, Stephanie Barahona, Suji Jeong, Longen Lan, Rosemary Menzies, Tracy Trieu, and Ann Wen. 2017. "In Conversation Together: Student Ambassadors for Cultural Competence." *Teaching and Learning Together in Higher Education* 21: 1-8. http://repository.brynmawr.edu/tlthe/vol1/iss21/5.

Cook-Sather, Alison, Cathy Bovill, and Peter Felten. 2014. *Engaging Students as Partners in Learning and Teaching: A Guide for Faculty.* San Francisco, CA: Jossey-Bass.

Dunne, Elisabeth, and Roos Zandstra. 2011. *Students as Change Agents: New Ways of Engaging with Learning and Teaching in Higher Education.* Bristol, UK: ESCalate, HEA Subject Centre for Education. http://escalate.ac.uk/downloads/8242.pdf.

Foundation for Young Australians (FYA). 2017. "The New Work Smarts: Thriving in the New Work Order." https://www.fya.org.au/report/the-new-work-smarts/.

Healey, Mick, Abbi Flint, and Kathy Harrington. 2014. *Engagement through Partnership: Students as Partners in Learning and Teaching in Higher Education.* York, UK: Higher Education Academy. https://www.

heacademy.ac.uk/knowledge-hub/engagement-through-partnership-students-partners-learning-and-teaching-higher.

Matthews, Kelly. 2016. "Students as Partners as the Future of Student Engagement." *Student Engagement in Higher Education* 1(1): 1-5. https://sehej.raise-network.com/raise/article/view/380.

Matthews, Kelly, Alexander Dwyer, Lorelei Hine, and Jarred Turner. 2018. "Conceptions of Students as Partners." *Higher Education* 76, no. 6 (December): 957-71. https://doi.org/10.1007/s10734-018-0257-y.

Peseta, Tai, Amani Bell, Amanda Clifford, Annette English, Jananie Janarthana, Chelsea Jones, Matthew Teal, and Jessica Zhang. 2016. "Students as Ambassadors and Researchers of Assessment Renewal: Puzzling over the Practices of University and Academic Life." *The International Journal for Academic Development* 21 (1): 54-66. https://doi.org/10.1080/1360144X.2015.1115406.

Pizzica, Jenny. 2018. "Partnership Pedagogy." Resource from the 21st Century Curriculum Project Learning Transformations Western Sydney University. https://www.westernsydney.edu.au/__data/assets/pdf_file/0006/1445289/PP2_pager_v2.1_120818.pdf.

Price Waterhouse Coopers (PWC). 2014. "The Future of Work: A Journey to 2022." https://www.pwc.com.au/pdf/future-of-work-report-v23.pdf.

Sabri, Duna. 2011. "What's Wrong with 'The Student Experience'?" *Discourse: Studies in the Cultural Politics of Education* 32, no. 5 (December): 657-67. https://doi.org/10.1080/01596306.2011.620750.

Williams, Jeffrey J. 2008. "Teach the University." *Pedagogy* 8, no. 1 (Winter): 25-42. https://muse.jhu.edu/article/229021/pdf.

CHAPTER 7

The Experience of Partnerships in Learning and Teaching

A Visual Metaphor

Kelly E. Matthews
Associate professor
University of Queensland
Australia

I like the idea of messing with assumptions about what it means to be a *student* and a *teacher*; questioning taken-for-granted ways of thinking, being, and relating in education. I prefer to work *against the grain* (Bad Religion circa 1990). So, the versions of engaging in pedagogical partnership that enable an *unlearning* of neatly defined student-teacher boundaries resonate with me.

But what is partnership?

The language of "student as partners" startles most people when they first come across it. It invites further dialogue as productive metaphors do. It asks us to unlearn what we think we know. It provokes us into self-reflection that destabilizes neat "student/teacher" categorizations that tend to dehumanize through abstraction.

The stories to name and describe what I am *unlearning* through pedagogical partnerships come easily. Naming what I am *learning*, experiencing, feeling, understanding by aspiring to be and relate with others through partnership in my teaching and learning praxis stretches my capacity to communicate. My words to communicate this partnership thing read like:

Engaging in learner-teacher partnerships in hierarchical educational structures is messy work fundamentally about human relationships in a particular socio-cultural context. Power and identity always come into the story of pedagogical partnerships. It is a way of thinking, being, and relating in higher education as human beings who care about other human beings.

Used with permission from the artist, the always thought-provoking Alex Iktan Ponce-Matthews

Sometimes I just say:

It is messy. Messy like this picture. An artwork to communicate what my words struggle to communicate about pedagogical partnership—the beautiful, chaotic, and colorful messiness that is my experience of this thing I call teaching and learning partnerships.

What I am currently appreciating about the whole partnership thing is that it is messing with what we do in higher education. By messing with what we do, the idea—the language itself—is creating space to think together. Importantly, this space includes a group of people—students—typically excluded from the learning and teaching conversations that carry the weight of making decisions, guiding action, and shaping policy.

In the spirit of this book's intention to "break the mold" of "traditional academic formats," I offer my insights into partnership through a visual metaphor. An image I present regularly to enrich my inadequate words. An image that is messy: untidy, confused, and difficult to name or describe. An image that makes some people uncomfortable, while others react with relief and some express confusion because a hard-to-name thing is captured. An image to capture a different imagination of being in a learner-teacher partnership. An image to *create space* for a different kind of conversation about what it means to embrace the version of partnership that appeals to me. An invitation to hear other versions of partnership.

Revolutionizing higher education is the intimate, personal act of dialogue embracing difference. Thinking differently about partnership, as more than words—as art—can open up different forms of dialogue. This particular visual metaphor is about the messiness of human relationships that, for me at the moment, define how I am making sense of pedagogical partnership. An image, I contend, that offers space to affirm the messiness of an idea, an aspiration, a practice, a pedagogical praxis, and a commitment. So, I ask you:

How is your partnership messy?

CHAPTER 8

On the Edge

The Spaces Between Student-Staff Partnerships

Amani Bell
Associate professor
University of Sydney
Australia

Stephanie Barahona
Honours candidate
University of Sydney
Australia

Bonnie Rose Stanway
Doctoral researcher
University of Sydney
Australia

This chapter is a collaboration between an academic (Amani), a PhD student who is also a member of staff (Bonnie), and a recent alumna (Stephanie) who all have been involved in student-staff partnerships at our institution. We met in one of the university's iconic and historic spaces—the Tudor Gothic style Quadrangle building constructed in the nineteenth century—to have a conversation about our involvement in student-staff partnerships. It was hot day, and the high-ceilinged, white-walled room was crowded with chairs and desks. We found a little corner where we could chat. This chapter captures our conversation and is illustrated by Stephanie.

Amani: When I looked at Alison Cook-Sather's book (2006, 135-36), she talked about spaces of imagination created by educational practices. I thought it'd be good to use some of her ideas as prompts for our conversation. I'll just go through them, and then we can decide where we want to start. Alison outlines: creating new spaces of imagination and action between and among participants; between and among disciplines; between what is considered personal and what is considered academic; outside of the spaces and the flow of time to which participants were accustomed; and that challenge participants to address differences of language and how those differences constitute and open up spaces between and among them.

With this last one, I was thinking about the language of academia and how students encounter that but also language in Bonnie's WeChat project.

Steph: They're very interesting things—yeah.

Amani: Another one of the prompts is highlighting juxtapositions between academic selves and student selves—between past and future selves. We've all been students. Bonnie currently is a student. Steph has very recently been a student and is now moving on to other roles. So, it's talking about our past and future selves. Can we talk about those prompts? Is there a particular one that you think would be good to start with?

Bonnie: How about we start with that last prompt, which is about identity. What I find interesting here is that different people play different roles in student-staff partnership projects. Often this is determined by the intersection of *how* and *when* people are coming together to collaborate. I technically wasn't a student at the beginning of our project last year. I'd finished my masters, and I hadn't yet started my PhD, so in the eyes of our student partners, I was very much a member of staff. But during the project, I became a PhD student as well. So our "official" roles or identities change over time.

That's what I struggle with a bit with regards to the students as partners concept. The concept includes these predetermined roles—students and non-students—but those can change over time. Partnership is a very fluid relationship, and it can change based on what projects you're working on and who you're working with. I think this is an important thing to call out at the beginning of our conversation because there are different times and spaces where you choose what role you're going to play and who you're going to be in the partnership. Or perhaps those roles choose you.

Amani: For me, there's something between the present and past self. It always brings up a lot of memories and emotions of being a student when I work with students as partners. But I also try to be cautious not to superimpose those experiences on what students are experiencing now because my experiences were a long time ago. It pulls me into an in-between space, between being student and staff.

Steph: As a student, I felt as though I was living in some sort of purgatory—in the sense that I was experiencing academia between two worlds. I was a student assisting an academic who was trying to help student partners develop modules for their fellow students. It was quite an interesting experience simply because I was looking in from the outside (Leung, Barahona, and McDonnell 2017). In those moments, I didn't feel like I was a student per se. It was a weird space to be in, but a very rewarding one in the end because you're contributing to the future of these partnerships between students and academics. Going to university can be a very isolating and uncomfortable experience, and when you have an academic who is willing to hear all your concerns, it can be a really heartwarming thing. I often think back about the projects we did, and I feel so lucky to have had these experiences.

Amani: Can we come back to that? You mentioned it was kind of uncomfortable being in that in-between space.

Steph: I did feel a little uncomfortable because I was the only student taken to a conference and I didn't really know what to expect. I was taken through a portal into the academics' universe. So, naturally, I did feel intellectually and socially insecure because of the inherent power dynamics at play. However, over time, I saw how vital my role was in constructing this project because, by the end of it all, the student partners all expressed a universal feeling of like "*oh, I'm so glad I did that. I learned so much. I can apply all the skills that I've learned here for my career.*"

Bonnie: The best of both worlds. This intersection is something that could be interesting to share our stories about because, in that in-between space, you can access both worlds. This does mean, though, that you often have to go through an awkwardness of crossing an uncomfortable or challenging threshold to grow from the experience (Cook-Sather 2014; Marquis et al. 2016).

Amani: It reminds me of that film *Arrival* (Levy et al. 2016), where the aliens arrive on Earth, and the main character is a linguist. She has to work out the alien language, and the aliens are working out human communication.

Bonnie: Which ones are the students?

[Laughter]

Amani: They have that in-between space where they meet in the spaceship. The humans go up into this environment where there's a translucent screen between the humans and the aliens. That's where the communication happens: in the in-between world. But the humans don't understand the aliens fully until they go right up to and eventually past the screen. There's a point where the linguist just takes off all her protective gear and says, *"They need to see me."* She looks up and sees that the aliens are much bigger than she realized. Before they just looked like these tentacular legs, but now she sees they're actually these huge beings, and she has a more genuine communication. Now, I'm not saying that academics are aliens . . .

[Laughter]

. . . or that students are aliens in this situation either. But I did like that imagery of the in-between space of meeting, but then you have to go beyond your comfort zone to really understand each other.

Steph: You mentioned translation and comfort zones which reminded me of Sofia Coppola's *Lost in Translation* (2003) where two strangers meet in a foreign city in a short amount of time, and they just happen to get along so well. That's what I felt actually. In the partnership team, we

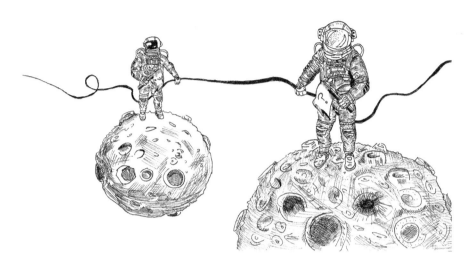

developed a shared language, and we intuitively understood the importance of our project, much like Charlotte and Bob interacting with each other within the landscape of a foreign city.

Amani: That idea of the languages of academia and students must have been even more extreme for you, Bonnie, in your WeChat project (Stanway et al. 2019). Could you say a bit more about language and the in-between spaces of that project?

Bonnie: Yes! Language was important on many levels. There was the aspect of translation between students' and academics' worlds, but then we were working with international students, so there was also a whole set of other linguistic, cultural, institutional, and hierarchical norms that we were navigating through and around. On a practical level, we were also enhancing the international student partners' English language skills through working on these projects. And, of course, students were teaching us about a completely different WeChat language that we didn't know much about.

Language was also interesting because we were working in an in-between space where we were looking at Chinese literature for the project, which only the student partner could tell us about because she spoke Chinese and the academics didn't. So, there was this whole layered translation effort going on and many different spaces that we were playing in.

Amani: So, there were several different spaces in-between—between the various languages, between students and staff, between generations, between cultures, and between hierarchies. Did you go through different stages of working through discomfort together—how did it all play out?

Bonnie: Everyone was coming across something new or different all the time. Instead of being in the dark about it, and not knowing what to do, we'd established these relationships where we could ask each other. Student insights meant we didn't need to go through a trial and error process. We had advisors on this unknown world, and they guided us until we knew more and felt more comfortable in that space.

Amani: For students, the language of academia can be uncomfortable. The language academics use does not invite students into that space. For example, we had the annual teaching colloquium [an internal learning and teaching conference] (Peseta et al. 2016), and some of the student partners said, *"What's a colloquium? That doesn't sound like somewhere that students are welcome to go."* Academics need to think more about the way they make the spaces inviting. I think the partnership project was that in-between space where the student partners became more comfortable entering what was initially an academic space, and that space became co-created and co-owned.

Steph: Student-staff partnerships are the gateway to creating a common language between academics and students, which is something that Cook-Sather and Abbot have also found (2016). With you and Tai [Peseta], I felt really comfortable because you were both accommodating and supportive, so I didn't feel like I was completely alone or like an "alien." Semantics are important, and we can develop a language that we both understand—that we can both work with.

Amani: Something you did at the beginning, Bonnie, which I think helped create that productive in-between space was to have an explicit conversation about the values of partnerships. What do you feel that achieved?

Bonnie: I think the explicit conversation about partnership values was crucial to the success of our project. At our first project meeting, we had a session with Amani where we ran through what a student-staff partnership is like when it comes to research and practice.

As part of that, we had a discussion around the Higher Education Academy (2016) partnership values. Having that conversation right at the start and deliberating on a couple of the values was crucial. It set the partnership framework from which we were going to operate. The values were always there in the back of everyone's minds.

The project team talked about that session a lot. Having that session right at the beginning was good because we were able to foresee where the tensions might arise in the partnership. For example, how do you give authority to students in a university situation where staff are supposed to be the authority? We were able to explore and address these tensions from the beginning, and it meant that when challenges came up later, we navigated through them more easily. We knew that we were aiming to operate with these values, and we would try really hard to stick to them.

Amani: What about between and among disciplines? That's another kind of space that we've been working in. Do you have any thoughts about how that played out in the projects?

Bonnie: It reminds me of the edge effect concept, where if you're so deep into an idea or a discipline it can be hard to question and challenge it because you might just be in too deep. Being on the edge allows you to reflect back on your own practices—on the practices of colleagues and peers. Being in a student-staff partnership allows you to be on the edge, and to work with other people who are on the edge, and to have that productive self-reflection.

Amani: [Reading out a quote] "Many species seek out edges because they offer simultaneous access to multiple environments and a greater richness in habitat" (Digitally Engaged Learning 2018). It's richer at the edge.

Steph: What an image!

Bonnie: I really like that.

Amani: Another prompt was between what is considered personal and what is considered academic. Do you think these kinds of spaces had that quality?

Steph: I think they did. We brought our own personal stories (University of Sydney 2015), and I think in retrospect they were quite necessary to the research because we all came from different backgrounds, like me being a low socioeconomic status student. We have all faced our own sorts of struggles. So those stories were necessary to analyze the diverse student experience because the university can be a very tough place to navigate, especially if you're not from the North Shore [a wealthy area of Sydney], if you don't have rich parents, and so whenever we had our meetings I felt like I could talk about my experience. Personal stories are very important in developing this language and this space.

Amani: There was a prompt about outside of the spaces and the flow of time to which we are accustomed. These initiatives do take time—time to develop the relationships and understandings. But there's a paradox between the idea of a project which ultimately is short-term and has an end date—whether that's through a time frame or through funding or whatever—yet student-staff partnerships are about relationships, and those relationships transcend a finite date of a project.

Those initial projects have finished, but Steph and I are still in contact. We're working on this chapter now, which is great. Ideally, it's an ongoing relationship. The other thing that's outside the normal flow of student time is publications. Publications can take a long time, and in some cases, it's after the students have graduated.

Bonnie: Also, student partners are given the opportunity to become experts while being engaged in the student-staff partnership. They build up a great knowledge base, but if they want to continue working in that area—either on research or for professional development—this can often extend well beyond what is initially stated in a project proposal. We're in regular contact with our students post-project. This week we had positive feedback from reviewers on our co-written article, so of course, I reached out to them. One of them is working in industry now, but they are still offering to help and be a part of it, and that's well beyond the life of the project.

Steph: I feel that way too. The skills that I've gained from these projects are very transferable. I'm interning at an art gallery at the moment, and they are trying to dismantle the structures that prevent young people from accessing art. It's something close to my heart because when I was a teenager, I wanted to be an artist. Looking at it from the "edge," it's interesting to see that there are people out there who are willing to create these spaces where we can meet eye-to-eye about these issues revolving around socioeconomic access to culture and art.

Bonnie: I'm just thinking about the space concept, and I feel like we've talked about how the people creating that space are important, but the physical space is important too. I remember when we brought students in for our first team meeting. It was in a meeting room behind closed doors, accessible only by using a staff swipe card. They had to knock on the door. Staff had to let them in. This is so different from the physical meeting space being an accessible open environment, such as a café. As the students walked through the security door into this meeting room, I think that alongside the potentially unwelcoming impression, they realized that entering into this space they were now in a position to be able to learn more about the institution and how it works, behind the scenes. In this way, the physical space that a partnership plays out in can have multiple and unintended impacts on student and staff partners. This is true of the historical, traditional education space where we are having this conversation right now—we're challenging the traditional space by talking about innovations and intersections.

Steph: I appreciated the discomfort, the awkwardness of being in-between and being on the "edge" because I knew that ultimately it would be worth going through it all to push through to get to the other side.

Amani: It's a brave space. It's getting away from the idea of a safe space. You can never create a truly safe space for everyone. But you can create a brave space (Arao and Clemens 2013). So I think we're saying that working in this way is not all roses—it's not always positive and amazing. It is risky, but in the end, it is more fruitful than if you didn't work in this way.

Bonnie: Risky and rewarding. R&R . . . It's the opposite of the other R&R . . . rest and relaxation [smiling].

[Laughter]

Reflection Questions for Readers

- We have found it valuable to use pop culture references and metaphors to describe student-staff partnerships. What other pop culture references and metaphors came to mind as you were reading? If you wish, please share your observations on Twitter using the hashtag #studentsaspartners.
- We have included illustrations in this chapter. If you sketched your experiences with, or feelings about, student-staff partnerships, what would that look like?
- In our conversation, we discuss several interstices—spaces between—in partnership where new possibilities emerge and traditional barriers are overcome, for example, language, time, identities, and disciplines. What are some other in-between spaces in student-staff partnerships?

References

Arao, Brian, and Kristi Clemens. 2013. "From Safe Spaces to Brave Spaces: A New Way to Frame Dialogue around Diversity and Social Justice." In *The Art of Effective Facilitation: Reflections from Social Justice Educators,* edited by Lisa M. Landreman, 135-50. Sterling, VA: Stylus.

Cook-Sather, Alison. 2006. *Education Is Translation: A Metaphor for Change in Learning and Teaching.* Philadelphia: University of Pennsylvania Press.

Cook-Sather, Alison. 2014. "Student-Faculty Partnership in Explorations of Pedagogical Practice: A Threshold Concept in Academic

Development." *International Journal for Academic Development* 19 (3): 186-98. https://doi.org/10.1080/1360144X.2013.805694.

Cook-Sather, Alison, and Sophia Abbot. 2016. "Translating Partnerships: How Faculty-Student Collaboration in Explorations of Teaching and Learning Can Transform Perceptions, Terms, and Selves." *Teaching & Learning Inquiry* 4 (2): 1-14. https://doi.org/10.20343/teachlearninqu.4.2.5.

Coppola, Sofia, and Ross Katz (Producers) and Sofia Coppola (Director). 2003. *Lost In Translation.* Motion Picture. USA: Focus Features.

Digitally Engaged Learning. 2018. "About the Conference." http://www.digitallyengagedlearning.net/2018/about/.

Higher Education Academy. 2016. "Framework for Student Engagement through Partnership." https://www.heacademy.ac.uk/system/files/downloads/student-enagagement-through-partnership.pdf.

Leung, Natalie, Stephanie Barahona, and Michael McDonnell. 2017. "Understanding Student Awareness of Their Cultural Competence Skills in the Humanities." http://sydney.edu.au/education-portfolio/ei/teaching@sydney/understanding-student-awareness-cultural-competence-skills-humanities/.

Levy, Shawn, Dan Levine, Aaron Ryder, and David Linde (Producers) and Denis Villeneuve (Director). 2016. *Arrival.* Motion Picture. USA: Paramount Pictures.

Marquis, Elizabeth, Varun Puri, Stephanie Wan, Arshad Ahmad, Lori Goff, Kris Knorr, Ianitza Vassileva, and Jason Woo. 2016. "Navigating the Threshold of Student-Staff Partnerships: A Case Study from an Ontario Teaching and Learning Institute." *International Journal for Academic Development* 21 (1): 4-15. https://doi.org/10.1080/1360144X.2015.1113538.

Peseta, Tai, Amani Bell, Amanda Clifford, Annette English, Jananie Janarthana, Chelsea Jones, Matthew Teal, and Jessica Zhang. 2016. "Students as Ambassadors and Researchers of Assessment Renewal:

Puzzling Over the Practices of University and Academic Life." *International Journal for Academic Development* 21 (1): 54-66. https://doi.org/10.1080/1360144X.2015.1115406.

Stanway, Bonnie Rose, Yiyuan Cao, Tony Cannell, and Yihui Gu. 2019. "Tensions and Rewards: Behind the Scenes in a Cross-Cultural Student-Staff Partnership." *Journal of Studies in International Education* 23 (1): 30-48. https://doi.org/10.1177/1028315318813199.

University of Sydney. 2015. "Cultural Competence Is Our Business Too! — Student Ambassadors." Filmed November 2015 at The University of Sydney. Video, 31:48. https://youtu.be/nd-5IwCX-cY.

CHAPTER 9

A Radical Practice?

Considering the Relationships between
Partnership and Social Change

Rachel Guitman
Undergraduate student
McMaster University
Canada

Elizabeth Marquis
Assistant professor
McMaster University
Canada

Healey, Flint, and Harrington define student-faculty partnership as "a *process of student engagement* . . . in which all participants are actively engaged in and stand to gain from the process of learning and working together" (2014, 7). They also propose authenticity, inclusivity, reciprocity, empowerment, trust, challenge, community, and responsibility as underpinning principles for their conceptual model of partnership. Based largely on these principles, partnership has frequently been framed as a practice with transformative potential (Matthews, Cook-Sather, and Healey 2018; Healey, Flint, and Harrington 2014; Cook-Sather 2014). It has also been positioned as a radical approach, with the terms "radical collegiality" (Fielding 1999, 3; Bovill, Cook-Sather, and Felten 2011, 133) and "students as radical agents of change" (Fielding 2001, 123) being used to describe it and related practices. Although this is certainly not exclusively how partnership has been viewed, we are interested in thinking here about partnership as a radical, political practice. We explore its potentials and limitations within that frame, whether or not it should be understood as political, and how connected it might (or should) be to efforts for social change.

Is Partnership Political?

> [There is a] false assumption that education is neutral, that there is some "even" emotional ground we stand on that enables us to treat everyone equally, dispassionately. In reality, special bonds between professors and students have always existed, but traditionally they have been exclusive rather than inclusive. (hooks [1994] 2014, 198)

Rachel: For me, the above quotation illuminates why partnership is a political process: it rests on a commitment to creating more inclusive professor-student bonds. Education always occurs in the context of a social world governed by politics, and it is a formative process connected to a student's existence as a political entity. As a student, I have experienced a pronounced shift in my political knowledge and conceptions at university, both from reflection in classes and through discussion and political activity with peers.

Paulo Freire and bell hooks both frame education as something that can never be apolitical; hooks writes that "the education most of us had received and were giving was not and is never politically neutral" (hooks [1994] 2014, 30). The movement for promoting students as partners is thus, to me, a political movement. When education and educational institutions are understood as inherently political, there is no such thing as apolitical "neutrality." Rather, there exists passivity that follows the "current" within the institution and the world; conscious or unconscious reproduction of norms; and active, intentional opposition to the status quo. Significantly, institutions and broader social power structures are typically hierarchical and often oppressive to people in marginalized positions, an idea both hooks and Freire discuss. As a result, any of the aforementioned ways of relating to these structures will always be political.

Partnership—at least in the ways that I have experienced it—falls into the latter category of intentional opposition to the status quo.

Beth: I agree that partnership is an inherently political process, Rachel. As you note, all education functions to support or destabilize the "existing state of things," while the extent to which postsecondary education institutions are currently shaped by neoliberalism, managerialism, and academic capitalism is hard to ignore. In this context, partnership *can* function as a means of pushing back and doing things differently; it is a process in which faculty and students are engaged as co-creators rather than purveyors and consumers of products (McCulloch 2009), and offers a re-humanizing space based in an "ethic of reciprocity" (Cook-Sather and Felten 2017, 176). I've certainly experienced this in many of my partnerships. While outcomes and deliverables may feature, the process is equally important: a huge part of the joy has been listening to and learning from one another. At the same time, scholars have noted the real potential for partnership to be understood in decidedly less radical ways. What are your thoughts about this possibility?

Rachel: This is something I have been thinking about frequently! Because partnership is a practice that typically happens within hierarchical institutions, it is not completely oppositional to those hierarchies. In fact, if one's concept of radical change means fundamentally dismantling institutions in their current form, then partnership does not constitute a radical practice. After all, how radical or transformative can partnerships be if they do not fully address the precarity, discrimination, and overwork common to their institutional settings? Do we lose something from the potential of partnership when those involved may be tangibly struggling to survive within institutions? I think that, in many ways, the answer is yes—when those involved must prioritize their survival, it may not feel possible to focus on radical change. These institutional issues mean that often it is only faculty in relatively secure, privileged positions who can reasonably become involved in partnership. I certainly think we lose out on a wealth of diverse potential perspectives when that's the case.

Beth: Your comments here also make me think about ongoing conversations about the possibility of partnership being appropriated for neoliberal ends. Mike Neary (2016), for example, has positioned partnership discourse itself as an example of the neoliberal university appropriating a more explicitly radical vision and making it safe by downgrading its subversive potential. In a discussion of the "Student as Producer" initiative at the University of Lincoln, Neary and Saunders (2016) illustrate how even a version of student-staff collaboration based intentionally on a model of militant Marxism and positioned "theoretically and practically as an insurgent form of higher education" (8) was ultimately "assimilated into the norms of academic life, so that its antagonism became a sort of fictitious competition" (13). Perhaps it's not then surprising that a recent study of senior leaders' perspectives on partnership (Matthews et al. 2018) documented a similar outcome: leaders viewed partnership largely through a neoliberal lens, emphasizing its potential to enhance the *educational product* on offer at the university and focusing largely on its overlap with student feedback and quality assurance measures. Such findings underscore that the politics of partnership are complex and that further attention to the interplay among its radical and conservative elements is essential.

Rachel: You're right that this is a significant tension; however, it does not mean that partnership does not deliver crucial value. Partnerships still occur against the backdrop of many forces pushing for neoliberal, transactional models of education (and of life). Although partnership might have limited "revolutionary" potential for fundamentally dismantling institutions, it is an essential pushback against the wider forces you have mentioned. It also creates alternate, often countercultural institutional environments that can allow other forms of radical resistance to flourish, even if it doesn't enact radical systemic change in itself. I have certainly felt partnerships to be spaces where I could be critical and political, and enact more change than in most other institutional settings.

A Diversity of Goals and Contexts: "Both/and"

Beth: Thinking about this further, I'm struck by the potential need for "both/and" understandings of partnership's political work. I see many ways in which the processes and outcomes of partnership might be viewed as simultaneously progressive and conservative—your example of individuals attempting to contribute to radical aims while also considering their survival in the academy is one example of this complexity. Here's another: I've been thinking lately of the emphasis, in some scholarship, on how partnership contributes to employability for student participants (e.g., Jarvis, Dickerson, and Stockwell 2013; Lewis 2017). This might be seen as an example of the neoliberal appropriation of partnership, or at least as a version of partnership focused more explicitly on congruence with (and lack of critique of) the university's role in the capitalist economy. At the same time, however, some research we've conducted at McMaster underlines that a large number of students are drawn to partnership programs precisely because they see these as potentially enhancing their capacity to meet future academic and career goals (Marquis et al. 2018b, 2018c).

Moreover, students who are not financially privileged may experience a need to focus on employment, a possibility which suggests that narrow critique of such motivations may itself be elitist and inequitable. If many participants come to partnership with (at least partially) non-radical goals in mind, and partnership is intended to honor the aims and perspectives of its participants, a challenge arises for those of us who might hope to underline partnership's radical potential. How do we respect the fundamental need to be responsive to participants while recognizing that those participants, like all of us, are influenced by the political realities in which we live and thus might not be (at least initially) interested in work that aims to destabilize existing practices?

Rachel: That's a really good point, Beth, that highlights why this tension is worth considering carefully. Even coming to a partnership with more radical goals in mind, I don't think anyone is removed from the material reality that means we must think about employability and academic progression. As a student, I was initially drawn to partnership for its underpinning ethos, but I also considered it a useful academic and career progression opportunity. Although I make a (privileged) choice to only get involved in extracurricular work that I genuinely care about, I always also think about that work's potential place on my resume, only because I operate in a context that makes me feel I **must** be advancing myself as a job/graduate school candidate while pursuing my degree.

Beth: The "both/and" issue also seems connected to the question of who participates in partnership activities. Some have rightly raised concerns that partnership opportunities are often made available only to small portions of the student population—and frequently to those that already experience various kinds of social privilege as a result of their identities and social locations (Felten et al. 2013; Moore-Cherry et al. 2016). Taking into account that partnership has been found to enhance student confidence and encourage a sense of belonging to institutions (Mercer-Mapstone et al. 2017), such limited access might, in fact, exacerbate existing inequities among students even while it works, progressively, to create new ways of being within the academy. In contrast, where opportunities to participate in partnership are available to students who identify as members of equity-seeking groups, the opposite outcome is likely. A growing number of studies demonstrate that partnership can contribute to equity by creating counter-spaces within inequitable institutions, enhancing equity-seeking students' confidence and valuing their knowledges and experiences (Cook-Sather and Agu 2013; de Bie et al. 2019).

Rachel: Absolutely. And opportunities for partnership that explicitly invite participation from members of equity-seeking groups make a powerful counter-hegemonic statement.

Beth: Nevertheless, the extent to which this is radical work can also be questioned. Creating spaces in which people feel welcome and valued within the academy is surely essential, but it could be argued that this does not function to meaningfully alter the structural injustices of the neoliberal university. In fact, like some policies around diversity and inclusion, it may dilute or provide ways to deflect calls for more pronounced change (see, for example, Kelley 2016). It's also worth thinking about the potential risks of partnership for members of equity-seeking groups. For example, it's well known that faculty occupying less privileged social locations experience a wide variety of injustices in the academy, including frequent challenges to their knowledge and expertise (Pittman 2010; Martinez, Chang, and Welton 2017). Might partnership, with its call to level hierarchies among staff and students and broaden notions of expertise, help to address this problem by explicitly valuing more expansive understandings of knowledge? Or, could it *exacerbate* these inequities by fortifying and sanctioning conditions in which equity-seeking faculty perspectives are questioned and undercut? Could it do both simultaneously? The potential for both/and outcomes in this regard remains a distinct possibility (see Marquis et al. 2018a).

Rachel: Definitely. The "both/and" possibilities highlight how much we stand to potentially gain, or lose, from partnerships. Do you think that partnership work can contribute to institutional or social change beyond the immediate contexts in which it is practiced?

Beth: Some research (e.g., Cook-Sather 2014; Cook-Sather and Abbot 2016; Marquis, Power, and Yin 2018) documents ways in which individuals translate the more egalitarian ways of being honed through partnership into a range of other pedagogical, professional, and personal experiences. Nevertheless, I've also heard people talk about how difficult it is to maintain a partnership approach in contexts that feel inhospitable to it, and I thus feel confident that translation doesn't always occur. To my mind, this is an issue that partnership has in common with the broader field of critical pedagogy in which it is rooted. As Rebecca Tarlau (2014) has argued, critical pedagogy as it developed within the US academy largely lost its connections to social movements and organizing, with the result that "critical pedagogues often fail to go from a 'language of resistance' to a theory of how people can form movements of resistance with that language" (369). As such, the potential for tangible social change is undercut. It seems to me that partnership, like critical pedagogy, might be doing much to lay the grounds for critical engagement and more democratic ways of being, but—without direct attention to translating those possibilities into resistant practice—its potential to foster meaningful institutional change is truncated. It becomes, potentially, a kind of prefig-urative politics—a hugely important liminal space in which people might try out and enact new ways of thinking and being (Matthews et al. 2018; Cook-Sather and Felten 2017), but one whose capacity to affect structures and systems beyond those spaces remains uncertain.

Partnership, Relationships, and Individuals

Rachel: I am also drawn to thinking about how partnership might poten-tially play into neoliberal models of education when it puts the focus on individuals and individual relationships, rather than larger systems and forces. I do think the relational aspect of partnership can be taken up in non-individualistic ways, but how partnership is often practiced and discussed in scholarly literature comes down to individual relationships. On the one hand, I think individual partnerships are crucial, and the ones I have been involved in have been hugely influential for me. Working with supportive, encouraging partners like you, Beth, has improved my confidence in myself and has promoted my growth as a scholar and leader. Clearly, individual interactions have great power to transform the expe-riences, worldviews, and feelings of individuals involved. That power is something I don't want to downplay because it is incredibly valuable. However, at the end of the day, a focus on individual relationships can only go so far in engendering institutional change, because that kind of change is not solely about individuals. It requires a collective effort and organizing, and there are many schools of thought (like postcolonial feminism or critical race theory) that reject the possibility of "radical" change without a fundamental rejection of existing structures. It can be dangerous to position individuals as agents of large-scale change because doing so can unfairly burden individuals with the mammoth task of changing the fundamental modes of functioning in an institution.

Beth: Absolutely. These comments remind me of a piece by Robin Kelley (2016), in which he argues that activists and others need to pay greater attention to structural issues as opposed/in addition to individual expe-riences in postsecondary education. Perhaps Kelley's reminder that "the personal is not always political" needs to be applied to considerations of partnership as well. At the very least, we ought to pay greater attention to the extent to which institutional structures support or discourage partnership work, rather than simply positioning it as an option for people to choose to take up. The issue of who takes part seems relevant here as well. If some faculty, for instance, are seen as particularly approachable by students or are especially committed to partnership's aims, they may end up spending a great deal of time engaging in partnership activities, which are not typically rewarded in questions of career progress. Partnership could, as a result, become akin to the "cultural taxation" experienced by racialized faculty in many higher education contexts (James 2012), not only putting the responsibility for change on individuals but also placing particular demands on those already marginalized in the academy.

Rachel: Despite the limits apparent in partnership as a mode of functioning *within* institutions, I still feel strongly about its necessity and benefit. Perhaps partnership does not need to be a completely radical, institutionally transformative concept or practice. Maybe an important distinction to make is between individual transformation and institutional transformation. Even without "overthrowing" current modes of institutional functioning, partnership still acts as a push against neoliberal universities, and any kind of move in the right direction is beneficial.

Beth: I also think it worth acknowledging that the relational focus of partnership can itself be understood as comparatively radical and resistant within higher education contexts focused emphatically on commodified outputs and products (Matthews et al. 2018). As Cook-Sather and Felten (2017) note, by emphasizing process and relationship rather than measurable outcome, partnership can counter techno-rational discourses and re-humanize higher education environments. This is another case where I'm left with a both/and argument, then, and a desire for greater discussion of partnership's potential and limitations.

Conclusion

We both remain excited by the many ways in which partnership has the potential to contribute to meaningful institutional and social change. Nevertheless, our discussion here has reinforced the fact that partnership is not *always*, *necessarily*, or *only* progressive, and that we, as a community of practitioners and scholars, would benefit from more nuanced and extensive consideration of its possibilities and limitations as a radical practice.

Reflection Questions for Readers

- Do you seek to make institutional change when engaging in partnership practice, and if so, what changes do you seek out?
- How might we create systems, structures, and processes that enhance partnership's capacity to contribute to institutional change? Should we?
- What might be an effective structure or strategy that could grow or support "counter-spaces" in your context?

References

Bovill, Catherine, Alison Cook-Sather, and Peter Felten. 2011. "Students as Co-creators of Teaching Approaches, Course Design, and Curricula: Implications for Academic Developers." *International Journal for Academic Development* 16 (2): 133-45. https://doi.org/10.1080/1360144X.2011.568690.

Cook-Sather, Alison. 2014. "Student-Faculty Partnership in Explorations of Pedagogical Practice: A Threshold Concept in Academic Development." *International Journal for Academic Development* 19 (3): 186-98. https://doi.org/10.1080/1360144X.2013.805694.

Cook-Sather, Alison, and Sophia Abbot. 2016. "Translating Partnerships: How Faculty-Student Collaboration in Explorations of Teaching and Learning Can Transform Perceptions, Terms, and Selves." *Teaching & Learning Inquiry* 4 (2). https://doi.org/10.20343/teachlearninqu.4.2.5.

Cook-Sather, Alison, and Praise Agu. 2013. "Student Consultants of Color and Faculty Members Working Together Toward Culturally Sustaining Pedagogy." *To Improve the Academy* 32, no. 1 (June): 271-85. https://doi.org/10.1002/j.2334-4822.2013.tb00710.x.

Cook-Sather, Alison, and Peter Felten. 2017. "Ethics of Academic Leadership: Guiding Learning and Teaching." In *Cosmopolitan Perspectives on Becoming an Academic Leader in Higher Education*, edited by Feng Su and Margaret Wood, 175-91. London: Bloomsbury.

de Bie, Alise, Elizabeth Marquis, Alison Cook-Sather, and Leslie Patricia Luqueño. 2019. "Valuing Knowledge(s) and Cultivating Confidence: Contributions of Student-Faculty Pedagogical Partnerships to Epistemic Justice." In *Strategies for Fostering Inclusive Classrooms in Higher Education: International Perspectives on Equity and Inclusion*, edited by Jaimie Hoffman, Patrick Blessinger, and Mandla Makhanya, 35-48. Innovations in Higher Education Teaching and Learning, Volume 16. Emerald Publishing Limited.

Felten, Peter, Julianne Bagg, Michael Bumbry, Jennifer Hill, Karen Hornsby, Maria Pratt, and Saranne Weller. 2013. "A Call for Expanding Inclusive Student Engagement in SOTL." *Teaching and Learning Inquiry* 1 (2): 63-74. https://doi.org/10.20343/teachlearninqu.1.2.63.

Fielding, Michael. 1999. "Radical Collegiality: Affirming Teaching as an Inclusive Professional Practice." *The Australian Educational Researcher* 26, no. 2 (August): 1-34. https://doi.org/10.1007/BF03219692.

Fielding, Michael. 2001. "Students as Radical Agents of Change." *Journal of Educational Change* 2, no. 2 (June): 123-41. https://doi.org/10.1023/A:1017949213447.

Healey, Mick, Abbi Flint, and Kathy Harrington. 2014. *Engagement Through Partnership: Students as Partners in Learning and Teaching in Higher Education*. York, UK: Higher Education Academy. https://www.advance-he.ac.uk/knowledge-hub/engagement-through-partnership-students-partners-learning-and-teaching-higher.

hooks, bell. (1994) 2014. *Teaching to Transgress: Education as the Practice of Freedom*. New York: Routledge. https://books.google.ca/books?id=z5wiAwAAQBAJ.

James, Carl E. 2012. "Strategies of Engagement: How Racialized Faculty Negotiate the University System." *Canadian Ethnic Studies* 44 (2): 133-52. https://doi.org/10.1353/ces.2012.0007.

Jarvis, Joy, Claire Dickerson, and Lewis Stockwell. 2013. "Staff-Student Partnership in Practice in Higher Education: The Impact on Learning and Teaching." *Procedia—Social and Behavioral Sciences* 90: 220-25. https://doi.org/10.1016/j.sbspro.2013.07.085.

Kelley, Robin D.G. 2016. "Black Study, Black Struggle." *The Boston Review*, March 7, 2016. http://bostonreview.net/forum/robin-d-g-kelley-black-study-black-struggle.

Lewis, David I. 2017. "Extracurricular Partnerships as a Tool for Enhancing Graduate Employability." *International Journal for Students as Partners* 1 (1). https://doi.org/10.15173/ijsap.v1i1.3052.

Marquis, Elizabeth, Rachel Guitman, Cherie Woolmer, and Elaina Nguyen. 2018a. "Identity, Social Location, and Staff Experiences of Pedagogical Partnership." International Society for the Scholarship of Teaching and Learning Conference, Bergen, Norway.

Marquis, Elizabeth, Ajitha Jayaratnam, Tianqi Lei, and Anamika Mishra. 2018b. "Motivations, Barriers, and Facilitators: How Students Perceive Student-faculty Partnership Programs." Society for Teaching & Learning in Higher Education Conference, Sherbrooke, Quebec.

Marquis, Elizabeth, Ajitha Jayaratnam, Anamika Mishra, and Ksenia Rybkina. 2018c. "'I Feel Like Some Students Are Better Connected': Students' Perspectives on Applying for Extracurricular Partnership Opportunities." *International Journal for Students as Partners* 2 (1): 64-81. https://doi.org/10.15173/ijsap.v2i1.3300.

Marquis, Elizabeth, Emily Power, and Melanie Yin. 2018. "Promoting and/or Evading Change: The Role of Student-Staff Partnerships in Staff Teaching Development." *Journal of Further and Higher Education*, July, 1–16. https://doi.org/10.1080/0309877X.2018.1483013.

Martinez, Melissa A., Aurora Chang, and Anjalé D. Welton. 2017. "Assistant Professors of Color Confront the Inequitable Terrain of Academia: A Community Cultural Wealth Perspective." *Race, Ethnicity, and Education* 20 (5): 696-701. https://doi.org/10.1080/13613324.2016.1150826.

Matthews, Kelly, Alison Cook-Sather, and Mick Healey. 2018. "Connecting Learning, Teaching, and Research Through Student-Staff Partnerships: Toward Universities as Egalitarian Learning Communities." In *Shaping Higher Education with Students: Ways to Connect Research and Teaching,* edited by Vincent Tong, Alex Standen, and Mina Sotiriou, 23-29. London: UCL Press.

Matthews, Kelly E., Alexander Dwyer, Stuart Russell, and Eimear Enright. 2018. "It Is a Complicated Thing: Leaders' Conceptions of Students as Partners in the Neoliberal University." *Studies in Higher Education,* June, 1-12. https://doi.org/10.1080/03075079.2018.1482268.

McCulloch, Alistair. 2009. "The Student as Co-Producer: Learning from Public Administration about the Student-University Relationship." *Studies in Higher Education* 34 (2) 171-83. https://doi.org/10.1080/03075070802562857.

Mercer-Mapstone, Lucy, Sam Lucie Dvorakova, Kelly E. Matthews, Sophia Abbot, Breagh Cheng, Peter Felten, Kris Knorr, Elizabeth Marquis, Rafaella Shammas, and Kelly Swaim. 2017. "A Systematic Literature Review of Students as Partners in Higher Education." *International Journal for Students as Partners* 1 (1). https://doi.org/10.15173/ijsap.v1i1.3119.

Moore-Cherry, Niamh, Ruth Healey, Dawn T. Nicholson, and Will Andrews. 2016. "Inclusive Partnership: Enhancing Student Engagement in Geography." *Journal of Geography in Higher Education* 40 (1): 84-103. https://doi.org/10.1080/03098265.2015.1066316.

Neary, Mike. 2016. "Student as Producer: The Struggle for the Idea of the University." *Other Education: The Journal of Educational Alternatives*

5 (1): 89-94. https://www.othereducation.org/index.php/OE/article/view/163.

Neary, Mike, and Gary Saunders. 2016. "Student as Producer and the Politics of Abolition: Making a New Form of Dissident Institution?" *Critical Education* 7 (5). https://doi.org/10.14288/ce.v7i5.186127.

Pittman, Chavella T. 2010. "Race and Gender Oppression in the Classroom: The Experiences of Women Faculty of Color with White Male Students." *Teaching Sociology* 38 (3): 183-96. https://doi.org/10.1177/0092055X10370120.

Tarlau, Rebecca. 2014. "From a Language to a Theory of Resistance: Critical Pedagogy, the Limits of 'Framing,' and Social Change." *Educational Theory* 64, no. 4 (August), 369-92. https://doi.org/10.1111/edth.12067.

SECTION THREE

GROWING PARTNERSHIP

SECTION INTRODUCTION

The Way of Partnership

Jenny Marie
Head of Quality Enhancement
Greenwich Learning and Teaching
University of Greenwich
United Kingdom

All around the globe, citizens of higher education embarked on a quest. They did so on the promise of a better future: one where they became fuller versions of themselves, empowered to be authentic, confident, passionate, articulate individuals in meaningful, trusting relationships with each other. And yet the terrain they had to cross was swampy—an uncertain, confusing, risky place that required courage and collaboration to stay their paths. The teachers had to shed their need for authority and control; the students needed to find their voice and agency. It was terrain they could not cross alone but only in the company of the other—for in sharing and listening and being there was the promise of understanding. Not all made it, for some the promise failed; but those that did saw differently and would never be the same again. They came to realise that partnership was a way of being, permeating our souls and changing the ways we learn and teach and relate; a way that lets us fully be.

As I read the chapters in the following section, I lost myself in their stories, conversations, poetry, pictures, and metaphors of growth. These chapters have distinct narrative qualities: they provide us with multiple actors who face loss and struggle; they portray uncertain situations, which are full of risk and promise; and they tell of a dream of a better future on the horizons of winding paths and tempestuous journeys. Sometimes the travellers reach their destinations; sometimes they fail. And yet, as chapter 14 (Jennifer Fraser et al.) explores, what is success and failure in partnership work? For even where the partnership "fails," the conversation is one of learning and growth.

The ambiguous/uncertain space which partnership traverses is discussed throughout this section. As Rumy Begum (chapter 14) says, "Here, it's different." This is a liminal space, full of possibilities as Anne Bruder (chapter 15) found, but also a risky, brave space. It is a place in which a path needs to be found. This may be successful; Rumy Begum describes how her partnership team "found our way," (chapter 14). But there is also the risk that partnership can become the "failed promise" that Alison Cook-Sather describes it being for her Māori colleagues (chapter 10). Sasha Mathrani (chapter 10) tells how she and her partner "seemed to be traveling on completely different paths," and Anita Ntem says, "I felt as though we were not on the same page" and that as a result, "I felt almost useless" (chapter 13). For them, there was no scarf across the table, offering a delicate path across the brave space, as in Abbi Flint's poem of chapter 11. And yet, Anita Ntem persevered and, for her, "all the moments of uncertainty, misunderstanding, and confusion, as well as careful attention, patience, and readjustment, had led to this moment of leadership" (chapter 13). Likewise, for Sasha Mathrani (chapter 10) the resistance she faced led to personal resilience and growth.

The relational nature of partnership is also raised across the chapters. Abbi Flint talks of partnership as "a way of being," "a way of relating" (chapter 11). Jennifer Fraser et al. (chapter 14) investigate the "processes of relationship building that are at the heart of student-staff partnerships," with Evgeniya Macleod speaking of the longevity of her partnership because "we made a connection," while Anna Dolidze speaks of the "friendships" created. With this relationship we hear multiple voices and, as Abbi Flint writes, "your voice / changes how I see" (chapter 11). For the voices to have power, we must be like Anne Bruder (chapter 15) and find ourselves listening without an agenda, and like Alison Cook-Sather, who "learned to listen anew to each voice, to know I would never know once and for all what students experience, think, feel, and know" (chapter 10).

Listening brings new understandings and new perspectives. For Anita Ntem (chapter 13) "partnership taught me to think differently," while for Fathimath Zuruwath Zareer (chapter 14) partnership work brought "a shift in perspective." Staff become vulnerable—as in Anne Bruder's story (chapter 15)—and in need of affirmation, as Anita Ntem (chapter 13) discovered. For Anna Dolidze, during partnership work, "you realize it's just another human being and we all make mistakes, we all get super excited about something, or super sad, and we all have burning questions" (chapter 14). This vulnerability lies at the heart of Desika Narayanan and Sophia Abbot's story in chapter 12. Sophia and Desika have both struggled with physics in the past, and Desika fears making mistakes in class. And yet, Sophia notices that when he does, this helps students to learn about common mistakes and creates a community where mistakes are okay. Together, they build a class based on community, trust, and honesty.

Partnership holds the "commitment to dreaming about a better world" for Evgeniya Macleod in chapter 14, and the possibility to "co-create alternative futures" for Abbi Flint (chapter 11). These better futures are both in terms of the education we provide and our own personal future. Partnership offers the chance for staff to be authentic and take off the mask of the expert, the teacher, the one in control and to be what Alison Cook-Sather (chapter 10) terms our "fuller selves," "a human being in relation to this world at this time." As I read chapter 15, I became enchanted by the idea that empowerment could come from the loss of control: in that case, Anne Bruder tells how she was freed from the need to act a part by ceding control to her students. She found that she had opened up space for authentically new ideas—she just needed to listen. For students, partnership offers, in addition to the employability skills Anna Dolidze mentions in chapter 14, what Sophia Abbot terms in chapter 12, "a strong sense of agency" and, as Sasha Mathrani writes, "an increased sense of confidence and ability to articulate myself," as well as "passion, and desire to effect change" (chapter 10).

Partnership can be a transformative journey, as can learning. Desika Narayanan and Sophia Abbot notice that the themes for the course they were improving were the same as those of their partnership: "clarifying expectations, pausing and checking in, and reassuring and acknowledging" (chapter 12). Anne Bruder found that good teaching was "changing the rules" and opening up "unexplored spaces," where students "worked in partnership with their classmates." She discovered that "in ceding a measure of authority, my students, in turn, incline toward authorizing themselves to direct their own learning" (chapter 15).

These themes raise the resounding question: is all good teaching a partnership?

CHAPTER 10

Discerning Growth

Tracing Rhizomatic Development through
Pedagogical Partnerships

Sasha Mathrani
Student consultant
Haverford College
United States

Alison Cook-Sather
Professor
Bryn Mawr College
United States

As a recent undergraduate student of biology and a current faculty member in education, our interests in the concept of rhizomatic development have different origins. We both find the concept particularly generative, however, in mapping our experiences of growth through participating in and facilitating pedagogical partnership. In this chapter, we describe our use of "rhizomatic" and share our experiences of partnership using three rhizomatic themes.

Orientation: Rhizomatic Development

The term "rhizome" is derived from Ancient Greek (*rhízōma* or "mass of roots"), and in biology, it is used to describe a horizontal underground stem that can send out both shoots and roots. Deleuze and Guatarri (1987) use the term "rhizomatic" to describe theory, research, and culture that allow for multiple, non-hierarchical entry and exit points, resist any kind of organization, move toward and fill available spaces but do not leave clear traceable paths, yet can constitute powerful and enduring growth.

Drawing loosely on both biological and philosophical understandings of rhizomes, and imitating these concepts in form, we write in associative, roaming ways about our experiences of pedagogical partnership. Although our experiences have unfolded in and through time, we do not aim to provide linear-sequential, cause-and-effect steps but rather to map a small number of the multiple branchings and connections that nurture forms of flourishing. The flourishing we discern in ourselves and others includes deeper understanding, increased confidence, greater clarity, and stronger convictions, all of which develop in different directions and at different rates.

We offer three rhizomatic themes that we call Upward-Growing Shoots, Nodal Relationships, and Barriers and Branchings. These reveal just a few of the forms of growth that make up larger non-hierarchical patterns of development—multiple, always spreading rhizomes that link across contexts and times, creating a largely invisible but deeply connected network of meanings and practices.

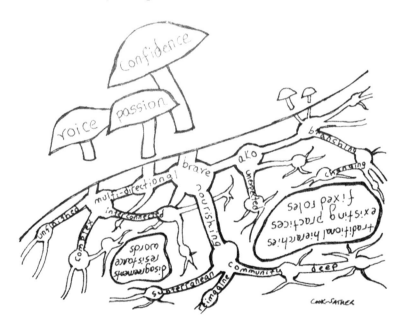

Illustration by Scott Cook-Sather

Upward-Growing Shoots

As the visual map of rhizomatic development above suggests, while most rhizomatic activity takes place under ground, invisible, some upward-growing shoots emerge above ground and become discernible. The shoots depicted in our map include voice, passion, and confidence, three of the most common we have discerned, but they also include the partnership program we developed itself and the way our work through it has informed other programs. Our stories below offer glimpses of how both these qualities and entities emerged for us.

Alison: The Students as Learners and Teachers (SaLT) program at Bryn Mawr and Haverford Colleges emerged out of multiple conversations born of ongoing, collaborative teaching and learning relationships. These conversations included questions, responses, possibilities, and rethinkings through dialogue among differently positioned people (students, staff, faculty) at the colleges (Cook-Sather 2018b). In the fall of 2006, administrators at Bryn Mawr College called for some sort of support for educational development for faculty but did not specify what kind. Several faculty members expressed a desire to make their classrooms more inclusive and responsive but did not have any set ideas about how to do that. Students articulated, neither for the first time nor for the last time, that there were multiple ways in which the institution did not see, recognize, or value their identities and knowledge. These multiple entry points into the conversation about what kind of program we might create yielded the growth of the student-faculty pedagogical partnership program that became SaLT as well as recommendations we regularly revisit and revise for how to make classrooms inclusive (Cook-Sather and Des-Ogugua 2018).

The students' words, in particular, have resonated with me ever since and inspire me always to keep listening. The details of what they had to say and the urgency, weariness, hope, and hesitation to trust that I heard in their tone still echo in my head. Listening to them then and perpetually, I learned to listen anew to each voice, to know I would never know once and for all what students experience, think, feel, and know and so would always want to make spaces to learn and to grow through that learning.

Sasha: Through my student-faculty partnerships, I developed an increased sense of confidence and ability to articulate myself (Mathrani 2018). These aspects of my growth have allowed me to engage in partnership outside the realm of my structured student-faculty partnerships. For me, partnership is engagement between student and faculty that pushes the boundaries of traditional hierarchies (Cook-Sather and Alter 2011; Crawford 2012; Mercer-Mapstone, Marquis, and McConnell 2018).

Throughout my time at Haverford, I engaged with a program working with local middle and high school students from backgrounds underrepresented in science. As a student coordinator for the program, I worked with various faculty and staff members who oversaw the program. Since these faculty and staff members served as my supervisors in this position, my relationship with them was different from the relationships I formed through pedagogical partnerships. The hierarchical relationship that I had with my supervisors in this position made it difficult to always be open and honest. However, over time I was able to use my position as student coordinator to push back against some of the fundamental structures of the program that existed because of a lack of thoughtful consideration of students' backgrounds and identities.

Although I was not always met with understanding and equal engagement, I developed resilience through the resistances I encountered, and other resistances in my traditional pedagogical partnerships (Ntem and Cook-Sather 2018). This resilience allowed me to continue to push back until I felt like my voice was heard. In my third year as a student coordinator for the program, the resistance I faced from the faculty and staff with traditional roles of power made it difficult to feel like my voice was heard. However, around the same time, a task force was convened to look at the program and evaluate its goals and structure. My passion for the program, increased confidence, and ability to articulate my views helped me to take on the role of a student representative on the task force. With a new avenue to voice my perspectives and space where I could continue to speak up, I stepped down as student coordinator and stepped into my role as a student representative. In this new space, I was no longer working within the traditional hierarchies of the program. Instead, I was in a space where my voice was emphasized. I received this personal communication from a faculty member who had initially resisted pushing the boundaries of traditional hierarchies.

> Hi Sasha,
>
> I just wanted to let you know how valuable I felt your contributions were to our task force discussion today. I know I was pretty quiet in the beginning, and that was deliberate. I was focusing on listening and taking notes, while also leaving room for you to share your ideas before jumping in (you know, the whole power dynamic thing). Sometimes, I think faculty don't give students enough time to develop their thoughts. I admire how comfortable you are in expressing yourself in a mixed setting like this committee.
>
> You are not afraid to engage deeply and with passion, which is so important! I hope that you will continue to be a role model for other students in this regard.

In reflecting on this experience, I found unexpected connections between my pedagogical partnerships and my work as a student coordinator. Through my pedagogical partnerships, I developed a sense of confidence, passion, and desire to effect change, and all of that growth transferred over to my experiences with this program. I was able to effect change in a way that I could not have foreseen. I am certain that through some pathway, my personal development through pedagogical partnerships grew beyond the traditional structures of partnership.

Nodal Relationships

In rhizomatic terms, a node is the part of the underground plant system from which roots and shoots grow. Represented in our map above by the knobby protrusions where multiple roots intersect, nodes are both connecting points and crossings. They are convergences of the qualities of pedagogical partnership nurtured through relationships, such as community and change. They are the sites of and a metaphor for growth.

Alison: The weekly meetings of student consultants that I facilitate in my role as director of SaLT provide nourishing conditions and nurture deep, multidirectional forms of relationship and growth. Over the last twelve years, I have convened more than a thousand such meetings. In these hours, student consultants and I meet as fuller selves than most of us feel we can be in other academic relationships. Under these conditions, we are at once teachers, students, and people with uniquely complex, intersecting dimensions of identity, all striving to multiply perspectives (Cook-Sather 2014) and to turn resistances into resiliencies (Ntem and Cook-Sather 2018). Together, we generate sustenance and imagine ways around impediments.

In turn, the relationships student consultants develop with their faculty partners are informed and guided by deep critical insight and the equally deep generosity of spirit student partners display as they work tirelessly to engage in meaningful ways, even when they express their exhaustion in those meetings. In the process of analyzing how best to develop classrooms that are productively challenging and inclusive of a diversity of students, we talk about what it means not only to be a pedagogical partner but also to be a human being in relation to this world at this time (Cook-Sather and Porte 2017). Perpetually mapping what can't be quite known, we try to complicate any either/or until it is a both/and. We strive to name what we experience as intersecting in any given node and work to find ways of holding the complexity, even as it sends shoots in new directions.

Sasha: After being in partnership with various faculty members, I have found that the course of each partnership is unique and unpredictable. The relationships that grew out of my partnerships were each special in different ways, but one stands out the most. In this partnership, my faculty partner and I reached a point in the semester where we seemed to disagree on different pedagogical practices. Our disagreements made our weekly meetings abrupt and uncomfortable.

During one of the weekly meetings, my faculty partner shared an idea he had for a class he was planning to teach the following semester: he wanted to start the class with a very difficult assignment to show the students they had a lot to learn. However, he said he did not want to tell the students the assignment was intentionally difficult. I felt uncomfortable with this idea, but our meeting ended with neither of us really seeing where the other was coming from. We seemed to be traveling on completely different paths. This meeting to me was a point in our partnership where I felt my partner and I might not be able to engage in difficult discussions—a sort of unexpected stopping point where we both felt too far from meeting at a common node.

After talking about this uncomfortable conversation in my weekly student consultant meeting, I had the chance to clarify for myself why I had not liked my faculty partner's idea. I was able to articulate that assigning intentionally difficult problems in class would deter students who were already doubting their place in the classroom—students from traditionally underrepresented backgrounds. I was nervous about bringing this up in my next meeting with him, but I gathered the courage to do so and shared my thoughts with him. When I clearly articulated the reasons behind my beliefs, my faculty partner seemed to become more receptive. I took a leap and ended up being affirmed in an unexpected way. This leap allowed my partner and me to create a "brave space" (Arao and Clemens 2013) in our meetings where we could have difficult discussions, disagree productively, and really engage with each other (Abbott 2016). This partnership ended in a strong relationship that grew out of a lot of uncertainty and discomfort. Although we had branched away from each other earlier in the relationship, we were able to converge at a common node that served as a site for growth.

Barriers and Branchings

The final phenomenon we represent in our map of rhizomatic development through pedagogical partnership is the barriers that roots and shoots may encounter, such as rocks in the soil, and how the roots and shoots must find their way around them, branching in new directions rather than continuing the way they were going. As we indicate in the upside-down text in the image, the kinds of phenomena that constitute barriers to partnership include resistances and disagreements, traditional hierarchies, existing practices, and fixed roles, and even words that we might think signal the same thing to different people but do not.

Sasha: In the spring of 2018, I accompanied Alison and a former student consultant to Muhlenberg College, where we engaged with students, staff, and faculty to imagine the possibilities of partnership within the culture and context of Muhlenberg. I entered the space with my conceptions of what partnership meant and how to enact effective partnerships. However, over my two days at Muhlenberg, I began to re-examine my understanding of partnership. In my experiences, partnerships were one-on-one relationships between student and faculty focused on re-examining a particular class or syllabus. The single story of partnership could have been a barrier to my growth. However, in conversations with students and faculty, I began to understand the culture of Muhlenberg, and I could see potential for partnerships in ways I had never conceived of. In a conversation with students, I heard the need for students' voices to be elevated in the community. Together we came up with an idea for students to run focus groups to document and share students' experiences, especially those of students with marginalized identities. Before going to Muhlenberg, I would never have conceptualized that idea as partnership. However, my conversations and interactions at Muhlenberg informed my changing definition of partnership, allowing it to branch around what could have been a barrier that stopped such growth.

Alison: I visit numerous institutions of higher education in many places in the United States and around the world. I am invited to share the pedagogical partnership approaches we have developed at Bryn Mawr and Haverford Colleges, and what I learn from people in these other contexts about their hopes, fears, goals, and plans prompts me to rethink my own. None so much as a visit to Aotearoa New Zealand in March 2018. I was excited about this trip because, two years before and leading up my visit, my host had begun to educate me about key principles of Māori teaching-learning, including *ako*, which means to learn and to teach through a process that is relational and social.

I heard so much resonance with pedagogical partnership principles colleagues and I (Cook-Sather, Bovill, and Felten 2014) had developed based on work done in the United States and the United Kingdom—respect, reciprocity, shared responsibility—that I was especially eager to be in dialogue with people in Aotearoa New Zealand higher education institutions. I was surprised when I learned that the word "partnership" evoked for some Māori colleagues failed promises made by the Crown traced back to the Treaty of Waitangi—the founding document of the country. It signaled the failures in the inequitable workings of an educational system that is more welcoming of and responsive to Pākehā (a Māori language term for New Zealanders who are of European descent) than to Māori and Pacific Islanders, the indigenous peoples of the country (Berryman and Eley 2017) (see Cook-Sather 2018a for more detail).

What do we do when sets of values share the same spirit, but the words that signal affirmation and empowerment in one context signal failed promises and disenfranchisement in the other? What do we do when we use the same terms without realizing we are talking past each other? That our cultural sets of values do not share the same spirit of intent? This is an exploration in which I am currently engaged with two colleagues in Aotearoa New Zealand, one Māori, one Pākehā (Berryman, Bourke, and Cook-Sather, in preparation). The growth I experienced in dialogue with these new colleagues extended in many directions, alongside and at branching angles to the directions in which I have been growing for years.

Un-ending

Rhizomes don't have beginnings and endings, they are always in the middle, in between things, interbeings. Each of the sprouts of growth we describe, some visible, mostly invisible, captures how pedagogical partnership recognizes the "radical unfinishedness of the human condition" and develops "our consciousness of this unfinished state" (Freire 1998, 100; see also Brunson 2018 and Cook-Sather 2006). To engage in and grow through pedagogical partnership, one has to be ready for unexpected, sudden branchings, knowing, as Anita Ntem, one of our student partner colleagues, has said, that there is no "right way" to go. Direction emerges from how we combine extending ourselves and being receptive to what comes toward us and how we work around the obstacles we encounter. The growth and change that come through pedagogical partnership are not always apparent at the time, but through reflection, they can be mapped backward, continuing that ever-branching rhizomatic growth.

Reflection Questions for Readers

- In what ways does the concept of rhizomatic development capture your experiences of pedagogical partnership and in what ways does it not work to characterize the kind of development through partnership you have experienced?
- Are there other concepts or metaphors that capture for you the experience of pedagogical partnership? What are they and what do they surface or highlight?
- What barriers have you faced in partnership, and how have you branched in new ways to grow around them?

References

Abbott, Clara. 2016. "Leaping and Landing in Brave Spaces." *Teaching and Learning Together in Higher Education* 18. http://repository.brynmawr.edu/tlthe/vol1/iss18/4.

Arao, Brian, and Kristi Clemens. 2013. "From Safe Spaces to Brave Spaces: A New Way to Frame Dialogue around Diversity and Social Justice." In *The Art of Effective Facilitation: Reflections from Social Justice Educators*, edited by Lisa M. Landreman, 135-50. Sterling, VA: Stylus Publishing.

Berryman, Mere, and Elizabeth Eley. 2017. "Succeeding as Maori: Maori Students' Views on Our Stepping Up to the Ka Hikitia Challenge." *New Zealand Journal of Educational Studies* 52, no. 1 (July): 93-107. https://doi.org/10.1007/s40841-017-0076-1.

Brunson, Mary. 2018. "The Formation and Power of Trust: How It Was Created and Enacted Through Collaboration." *Teaching and Learning*

Together in Higher Education 23. https://repository.brynmawr.edu/tlthe/vol1/iss23/2.

Cook-Sather, Alison. 2018a. "Perpetual Translation: Conveying across Cultural Contexts the Languages and Practices of Student Voice and Pedagogical Partnership." *Transformative Dialogues* 11 (3). http://www.kpu.ca/sites/default/files/Transformative%20Dialogues/TD.11.3_Cook-Sather_Perpetual_Translation.pdf.

Cook-Sather, Alison. 2018b. "Developing 'Students as Learners and Teachers': Lessons from Ten Years of Pedagogical Partnership that Strives to Foster Inclusive and Responsive Practice." *Journal of Educational Innovation, Partnership and Change* 4 (1). https://dx.doi.org/10.21100/jeipc.v4i1.746.

Cook-Sather, Alison. 2014. "Multiplying Perspectives and Improving Practice: What Can Happen When Undergraduate Students Collaborate with College Faculty to Explore Teaching and Learning." *Instructional Science* 42: 31-46.

Cook-Sather, Alison. 2006. *Education Is Translation: A Metaphor for Change in Learning and Teaching.* Philadelphia: University of Pennsylvania Press.

Cook-Sather, Alison, and Zanny Alter. 2011. "What Is and What Can Be: How a Liminal Position Can Change Learning and Teaching in Higher Education." *Anthropology & Education Quarterly* 42, no. 1 (March): 37-53. https://doi.org/10.1111/j.1548-1492.2010.01109.x.

Cook-Sather, Alison, Catherine Bovill, and Peter Felten. 2014. *Engaging Students as Partners in Learning and Teaching: A Guide for Faculty.* San Francisco, CA: Jossey-Bass.

Cook-Sather, Alison, and Crystal Des-Ogugua. 2018. "Lessons We Still Need to Learn on Creating More Inclusive and Responsive Classrooms: Recommendations from One Student-Faculty Partnership Program." *International Journal of Inclusive Education* 23 (6): 594-608. https://doi.org/10.1080/13603116.2018.1441912.

Cook-Sather, Alison, and Olivia Porte. 2017. "Reviving Humanity: Grasping Within and Beyond Our Reach." *Journal of Educational Innovation, Partnership and Change* 3 (1). https://dx.doi.org/10.21100/jeipc.v3i1.638.

Crawford, Karin. 2012. "Rethinking the Student/Teacher Nexus: Students as Consultants on Teaching in Higher Education." In *Towards Teaching in Public: Reshaping the Modern University*, edited by Michael Neary, Howard Stevenson, and Les Bell, 52-67. London: Continuum.

Deleuze, Gilles, and Félix Guattari. 1987. *A Thousand Plateaus: Capitalism and Schizophrenia*. Translated by Brian Massumi. Minneapolis: University of Minnesota Press.

Freire, Paulo. 1998. *Pedagogy of Freedom: Ethics, Democracy, and Civic Courage*. Lanham, MD: Rowman & Littlefield Publishers.

Mathrani, Sasha. 2018. "Building Relationships, Navigating Discomfort and Uncertainty, and Translating My Voice in New Contexts." *Teaching and Learning Together in Higher Education* 23. https://repository.brynmawr.edu/tlthe/vol1/iss23/6.

Mercer-Mapstone, Lucy, Elizabeth Marquis, and Catherine McConnell. 2018. "The 'Partnership Identity' in Higher Education: Moving from 'Us' and 'Them' to 'We' in Student-Staff Partnership." *Student Engagement in Higher Education Journal* 2 (1): 12-29. https://sehej.raise-network.com/raise/article/view/Mercer-Mapstone.

Ntem, Anita, and Alison Cook-Sather. 2018. "Resistances and Resiliencies in Pedagogical Partnership: Student Partners' Perspectives." *International Journal for Students as Partners* 2 (1): 82-96. https:// doi.org/10.15173/ijsap.v2i1.3372.

CHAPTER 11

Space in the Margin

The Poetry of Partnership

Abbi Flint
Educational developer and researcher
Abbi Flint Consulting
United Kingdom

On opening the book
I find the pages are filled
with paragraph after paragraph
of dense text, passive voice.
A reference list that spills
from covers to devour days.
Look here, you say, under *hegemony*
a spidery line tracks left
to pencilled notes, aslant.
There is space in the margin.

This hanging indent an invitation
      to prise the words apart
      shake loose the strokes of letters
      remake the text. All we must do
      is smooth down the paper and begin.

*Change begins
with the first question,
but who will ask it?*

Division

The student guide
at the university museum
tells me sponges
are just collections of cells
held together by bridges.

Press two through a sieve,
mix them up. It might look
a mess but they know
who they are. In the end
they return to their selves.

Is that how it is
when I try to see, to hear,
to learn as you?
The tidal pull of the self.
The impossibility of other.

Or is there a point
of unsettled balance,
a brackish suspension
free from shape's certainty
where all forms are possible?

To be another
for one swirling moment
and changed forever

Between us

Her e-mail suggests we meet
in the not-quite space
of the university cafeteria
to talk over coffee and cake.

Here, supervisions and group-work
rub tables with dissections of nights out.

She stands and waves.
I know her by the scarf
she often wears in class.
Blue and green geometric silk.

We sit down to our uncertain task.
A dance of asking, listening,
carefully offering slivers of self
between us
a brave space.

She pulls the scarf through her fingers.

Our work is built on words
and small actions:
a name remembered
a door held open
a palm outstretched
food shared.
Tiny significant kindnesses.

She lays her scarf across the table
between us
an intricate path.

Student or teacher
when creating the future
labels matter less

Growth

The seeds of these ideas
are planted but do not yet grow

> They require water
> and light
> earth to hold

> I am no nursery
> I am greening too
> supple as a sapling
> under this bark

> The path of my roots
> not yet set

We are both green shoots
and gardeners

*Like a flash of sun
cast through trees, your voice
changes how I see*

Where Next?

I hope that you enjoyed reading these poems and that they spoke to and with your experiences and ideas about partnership in some way.

> *How to start*
> *this uncertain task? Open doors*
> *may lead anywhere*

Before I close this chapter with my own reflections, I offer some questions which I hope will encourage you to consider how these (and your own poems) may open up new conversations around partnership.

Reflection Questions for Readers

- When reading these poems, was it a staff or student voice you imagined speaking? Does your reading of the poem change if you imagine the other voice as the "I"? What assumptions or ideas might this surface?
- How do the poems relate to your own understandings and experiences of partnership?
- How could you use poetry or other arts-based approaches in your partnership practice? For example: as a means of exploring the nature of partnership; as a way of sharing learning from partnership; as a research or evaluation method?

> *A question's power*
> *lies in the risk of asking and*
> *courage to listen*

Poetry itself can be a form of partnership, a dialogue between poet and reader (Keplinger 2016). I invite you to reflect on, respond to, and build on these poems in your own voice—perhaps by writing your own poems or another form of creative response.

Reflections on the Poetry of Partnership

I came to write this chapter as a student, writer, and reader of poetry, and as a scholar and practitioner of partnerships. I use the terms "student" and "scholar" here not to denote a specific status within higher education, but as spaces and roles I find myself inhabiting (often simultaneously) through my practice.

There are many reasons why I chose poetry as a way of writing about staff-student partnerships. Research poetry can be multi-voiced (Babcock 2017); it can weave together the voices of research participants, literature, and researcher. As an educational developer and researcher, I am interested in both the theory and practice of partnership. As a researcher, I am fascinated by how we understand partnership, and the interplay between these understandings, our beliefs about the purpose of higher education, and the nature of learning and working in the academy. As an educational developer, I'm interested in how we can create learning and teaching environments where partnerships flourish and how we support people to explore this way of working and learning together. Cultures and communities are shaped by the people who are part of them. This requires us to attend to the way partnership plays out in practice; how do individuals understand and embody this in the way they learn, teach, and work? Poetry can connect the conceptual and experiential aspects of partnership and may be a way of capturing and speaking across these multiple voices of theories, practices, and partners.

I understand partnership as a way of being in the academy; as a way of relating to one another and our experiences of learning and working in higher education. It describes a different mode of staff and students relating to one another than the traditional (often hierarchical) teacher-student relationship. In this way, it offers us a new language and lens to explore our experiences. Through this exploration, we can surface assumptions, challenge practices and policies that may restrict the nature of learning and teaching that is possible, and co-create alternative futures (Healey, Flint, and Harrington 2014). This enables different kinds of conversations about learning and teaching to emerge, and these conversations may benefit from being expressed through other forms than the traditional (if there is such a thing?) academic journal paper. Abegglen, Burns, and Sinfeld (2015) describe how new forms of writing (in their example, blogs) enabled student partners to "re-territorialize" and be playful within quasi-academic spaces. I am exploring poetry as a new space for my own scholarship, alongside other arts-based methods (Flint 2018).

Recently there have been calls to consider and write about the emotional aspects of partnerships (Felten 2017). Poetry may offer a way into this, through its capacity to share, engage, and connect through emotional experiences (Faulkner 2009).

Poetry often attends to the ambiguous and liminal. Similarly, some staff-student partnerships are located in the edgelands of academia, the betwixt-and-between spaces (Flint 2016). Outside formal teacher-student relationships, the roles and identities of partners can become opaque and less fixed (Jensen and Bennett 2016). It is perhaps here where the light that a partnership lens shines on higher education may be felt more keenly.

Morning birdsong
assembles many voices
to make music

The ideas explored in these poems are inspired by conversations with staff and students. They draw on my research collaborations and the work of others whose writing has enlightened and challenged my thinking. I appreciate the generosity and curiosity of these peers and scholars. Faulkner (2009) stresses the need for attention to form, craft, and effectiveness in research poetry. Each of the poems has been workshopped with other poets (for whose time and care I am also grateful).

My approach draws on: my experience as a poet; on research poetry (Babcock 2017; Faulkner 2009); and on how examples of poetry have been used to shed light on experiences of higher education and as a way of exploring and drawing together multiple research and historical strands (Carpenter 2017; Quinlan 2016). I am excited by the possibilities poetry offers for exploring and acknowledging the interweaving of the intellectual, practical, and emotional aspects of working and learning in partnership. Writing poetry is a method of inquiry into as well as writing about partnerships. For me, it is the beginning of an experiment.

References

Abegglen, Sandra, Tom Burns and Sandra Sinfield. 2015. "Voices from the Margins: Narratives of Learning Development in a Digital Age." *Journal of Educational Innovation, Partnership and Change* 1 (1). https://dx.doi.org/10.21100/jeipc.v1i1.148.

Babcock, Ashley. 2017. *Poet, Researcher or Both? Balancing Rigor and Creativity in Poetics Research.* SAGE Research Methods Cases. https://dx.doi.org/10.4135/9781473994768.

Carpenter, J.R. 2017. *The Gathering Cloud.* Axminster, Devon: Uniformbooks.

Faulkner, Sandra L. 2009. *Poetry as Method: Reporting Research through Verse.* Walnut Creek, CA: Left Coast Press.

Felten, Peter. 2017. "Emotion and Partnerships." *International Journal for Students as Partners* 1 (2). https://doi.org/10.15173/ijsap.v1i2.3070.

Flint, Abbi. 2018. "Un-fuzzing the Fuzzword: Reflections on Using Visual Methods to Explore Understandings of Student Engagement through Partnership." In Proceedings of the RAISE international colloquium on partnership. *Student Engagement in Higher Education Journal* 2 (1): 116-17. https://sehej.raise-network.com/raise/article/view/Bryson.

Flint, Abbi. 2016. "Moving from the Fringe to the Mainstream: Opportunities for Embedding Student Engagement through

Partnership." *Student Engagement in Higher Education Journal* 1 (1). https://sehej.raise-network.com/raise/article/view/382.

Healey, Mick, Abbi Flint, and Kathy Harrington. 2014. *Engagement through Partnership: Students as Partners in Learning and Teaching in Higher Education.* York, UK: Higher Education Academy. https://www.advance-he.ac.uk/knowledge-hub/engagement-through-partnership-students-partners-learning-and-teaching-higher.

Jensen, Kathrine, and Elizabeth Bennett. 2016. "Enhancing Teaching and Learning through Dialogue: A Student and Staff Partnership Model." *International Journal for Academic Development* 21 (1): 41-53. https://doi.org/10.1080/1360144X.2015.1113537.

Keplinger, David. 2016. "Expert Commentary." In *How Higher Education Feels: Commentaries on Poems that Illuminate Emotions in Learning and Teaching,* edited by Kathleen Quinlan, 186-89. Rotterdam: Sense Publishers.

Quinlan, Kathleen. 2016. *How Higher Education Feels: Commentaries on Poems that Illuminate Emotions in Learning and Teaching.* Rotterdam: Sense Publishers.

CHAPTER 12

Increasing the Participation of Underrepresented Minorities in STEM Classes through Student-Instructor Partnerships

Desika Narayanan
Assistant professor
University of Florida
United States

Sophia Abbot
Master's student
Elon University
United States

We began a pedagogic partnership in September 2014 exploring student engagement and participation patterns in an introductory astrophysics course at Haverford College in the United States. We returned to our work in early 2018 to reflect on our experiences and examine the data we'd collected. Several themes emerged in this reflection that tied together not only the goals we set for the course but also our partnership more broadly: clarifying expectations; pausing and checking in; and reassuring and acknowledging. These themes both implicitly and explicitly helped us create a classroom environment of inclusion and equity for all students. This chapter is our sense-making of those themes, and we share both individually and in collaboration. Throughout, we use the notes we took during our partnership as examples.

Context

Sophia's Beginnings

I first partnered with a professor during the second year of my undergraduate degree, when I was encouraged to participate in a program called Students as Learners and Teachers (SaLT). In this context, I observed my faculty partner's classes weekly, met one-on-one with them to share what I saw in the classroom through notes and other feedback, and met weekly with fellow student partners to reflect on my learning and practice framing feedback. The goal of the program is to make space for perspective sharing on the pedagogy of the classroom and provide real-time feedback for faculty on their teaching. For students, the opportunity to help shape a class and figure out ways to advocate for oneself and one's peers can be invaluable—and for me, this translated to a strong sense of agency in my interactions with all my professors. In my final year of undergrad, and my third year of SaLT, I got to partner with Desika on his class, Intro to Astrophysics. I had spent a lot of time in my prior experiences thinking deeply about voice and space in the classroom. I wondered how we could make classrooms more inclusive, and I developed a technique for myself of mapping the participation in a classroom to visually represent the ways people spoke to one another. So, I was both excited and scared to bring these interests and techniques to a partnership in astrophysics—an academic area that had always been a source of anxiety for me.

Desika's Beginnings

My partnership with Sophia was my first engagement in any kind of student-teacher partnership. This course was only the second one I had taught (ever), and it was a critical one for ensuring that prospective majors approached their upper-level classes with the appropriate foundation. I was terrified. At the same time, I was encouraged to participate in this partnership within the context of a broader partnership between Haverford College (where I was employed) and Bryn Mawr College called the Teaching and Learning Initiative (TLI). Alongside weekly meetings with other faculty (and a professor leading the course), a major part of the TLI program is the student-teacher partnership. After being paired randomly with Sophia, we quickly realized that several techniques we discussed in the context of increasing student engagement could be used to broaden the participation of underrepresented minorities in the class. At the time, we focused specifically on students that identified as women as the primary underrepresented minority group in the course, though there were also several students of color in the course. In retrospect, I wish we had thought a bit more carefully about quantifying the effectiveness of our methods on a broader range of students in the field, though, at the time, the weightiness of the new course, combined with attempting to raise participation inclusively, was the most I could handle as a junior faculty.

Clarifying Expectations

There was already a structure in place for us to begin our work together, which helped us start our partnership with clear expectations. After the first meeting, Sophia attended one of Desika's first classes to observe. We decided to focus our efforts on clarity in the class to ensure all students had equal access to the material, in spite of varied backgrounds in the field. Some students had a strong physics foundation because of their high school curricula, and others were studying this kind of science for the first time. We didn't want those students to feel they were already behind their peers. We were concerned that more well-prepared students in STEM fields might unknowingly marginalize students from weaker backgrounds (who have comparable talents) with a combination of their confidence and domination of the space; too frequently, under-preparedness goes hand-in-hand with marginalized student identities due to the inequitable distributions of resources in our society (Museus et al. 2011; National Academies of Sciences, Engineering, and Medicine 2016). It was an important goal for our partnership to level the playing field.

Broadly, we focused on two major methods for increasing clarity of material:

- Increasing the focus and energy of students; and
- Increasing the transparency of what Desika intended students to take away on a given day.

Maintaining a high level of energy and focus throughout the course was critical to ensuring a thorough understanding of the material. You can't learn if you aren't focused! Because the class was one of the first ones offered for the day, we acknowledged that students would often come in cold. The beginning of every class was therefore devoted to a brief (five-minute) recap of the relevant material from the previous lecture, followed by time for questions to warm up for the day.

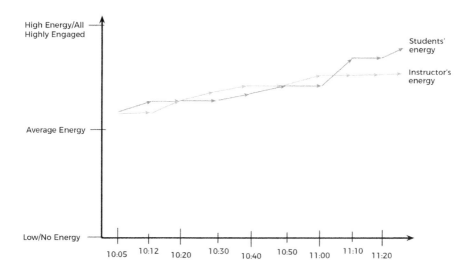

Throughout the lecture, energy naturally waxes and wanes. But in the mapping Sophia began to do (above), we noticed that there was a close relationship between Desika's energy and his students' energy. While this process wasn't especially scientific, Sophia did try to capture her general sense of Desika's and the students' energy levels through their body language, facial expression, and tone of voice. Critical to our efforts of maintaining high energy levels was constantly changing the pace of the lecture. Desika would often start with a walk-through of a relatively dry mathematical equation to explain the root of key physics concepts, under the premise that the students' capacity to focus was likely to be highest at the beginning of class. As Sophia noticed, however, very quickly students' eyes would glaze over. To help engage them, we worked on different types of questions that Desika could ask the class throughout the derivation. When Desika began to warn students of difficult or dry work coming up and clarify how hard derivations connected to broader themes of the class, students had the opportunity to develop their trust in him. In the same way that we practiced open communication in our partnership, Desika worked to foster that trust and reciprocity with students in the class. Their efforts to maintain focus and engagement reflect his trust in their capacity to do complex work.

In our second semester working together, Desika was especially intentional about the way he set the tone for his class of first-year students, as reflected in the following observation notes written by Sophia (with observations on the left and commentary on the right):

Observation	Commentary
8:00 – You talk explicitly about collaboration and the honor code. You use student names in your example. You say, "If you have any questions about your level of collaboration or resources, ask me."	This was something you were concerned about making clear. I think you did a great job of explaining what is appropriate and what is not. Your example was particularly helpful to me, both for understanding and for getting to know my classmates' names. You've set a great tone for the semester!
You explain your participation grading and say, "This is an activities-based class. Attendance is mandatory." You also explain what you mean by participation: "Not only that you are participating but that you are making sure everyone in your group has a voice . . ."	Thank you for noting this. I think it's something you may need to remind students of, but I'm so glad this was present in the first class. You were clear about your expectations that this classroom be a community and a supportive, collaborative learning environment.

You go over the topics to be covered and write them up on the blackboard.

You say, "If you don't think neutron stars are cool, then you don't know anything. They're the most awesome things!" And you explain.

Students are all highly engaged throughout, but especially here.

Your tone of excitement here is so engaging. Even I can't wait to return to talking about neutron stars, and for me the topics feel familiar from last semester!

Based on our prior semester of work together, Desika was also especially intentional about defining what he meant by participation: "Not only that you are participating, but that you are making sure everyone in your group has a voice." This distinction was born of something we struggled with in the prior semester: how to continue to show we value participation while balancing those students who may begin dominating the class discussion to the detriment of their peers? In the prior semester, some of this balancing began to happen naturally as Desika worked to create a community in his classroom, as described in the following notes:

Observation

A vocal student notices another student may have had a question as he's about to speak and says, "Wait, were you going to ask something?" The student says no.

Commentary

This is so great – even though the second student doesn't have anything to say, it indicates an awareness of peers that I haven't really seen before. Perhaps the group work is building class bonds?

The above exchange happened in November, about two-thirds of the way through the first semester. In large part due to Desika's intentionality and transparency about this goal, students seemed to do a much better job of accounting for one another in this second semester. It was thrilling to see the ways they began to create spaces for each other to participate, and the ways the students began to practice what Desika modeled for them in clarifying their intentions in their interactions with one another.

Pausing and Checking in

Early in our first semester, Sophia brought up the idea of checking in with the class mid-semester (in fact, we ultimately did three total check-ins with the class). Traditionally, Desika had used standard written evaluation forms that the students filled out. With Sophia's access and familiarity with the context through her observations, we were able to get significantly more meaningful feedback from the students in a facilitated conversation than the written medium alone provided. Pausing was important to us because we knew if we didn't check in with students early and often, we were far more likely to miss those who began to fall behind. We also hoped that asking for feedback would make students feel more comfortable approaching Desika at other times to share their thoughts or anxieties about the course.

Trust was an important aspect of the student-faculty partnership in adding to the value of the mid-semester check-in. By seeing one of their peers sitting in class weekly, as well as in Desika's office from time to time for our individual meetings, the students got to know Sophia as a quiet but regular staple of the course. As a result, we suspect they were more willing to open up to her than they might have been to others.

To start the evaluation process, Desika gave the students pre-written questions (the form he might have given them anyway had he not had access to a student partner), and then he left the room. The purpose of the written evaluations was to get them thinking about the course as a whole. After giving them time to write, Sophia engaged the class in a conversation for 15-20 minutes. While taking notes, she omitted any identifying information and specifics. Rather, what Sophia reported to Desika from the conversation were overall themes. How was his clarity? What more could he be doing to accentuate the delivery? How were the tests/homework? How did the students feel about class participation? The format of Sophia having a conversation with the students had several clear benefits. First, often one student would mention something, and it was clear through facial expressions and verbal responses that the rest of the class hadn't thought of that (and therefore would not have included it in their written feedback), but they agreed. The "pile-on" effect at that point would make it clear to Sophia that this was an actual issue in the course that Desika needed to address. On the other hand, if a student mentioned something and they were alone in their opinion, that too became clear. Second, larger themes were easier to capture as it was more obvious to Sophia sitting in a conversation what the repeated ideas were, which is something that can sometimes be harder to parse out in written evaluations. Finally, the conversational tone led to new ideas.

> Students mentioned that it can be hard to remember what different variables stand for when you're deriving long equations. One student mentioned that it would be helpful if you wrote a key of variables on the side of the board before going through an equation.

The example above shows the way students collaborated to offer feedback and suggestions. This particular suggestion improved the clarity of material so much that it's a technique Desika still uses today, four years later!

Students had the opportunity to develop trust in seeing Sophia regularly in class, and this was reinforced when Desika publicly responded to student feedback in class. In those moments—either seeing Desika take and apply a student suggestion or explain why a particular aspect of the course was necessary for student learning—students could see that the feedback process was genuine and their relationships with Desika were reciprocal.

Another method Desika adopted to shift energy and make space for new voices was to ask students to physically occupy different areas of the classroom. In the beginning of the semester as students developed patterns of seating and participation, we realized that if Desika asked a question and expected a response to come from a particular region of the classroom, he would look to that space. As that expectation became a habit, fewer and fewer students would participate because Desika's (and any instructor's!) natural fear of awkward silence would encourage him to seek out a reliable student. However, if students moved around the classroom semi-regularly, Desika would end up looking to different students to respond.

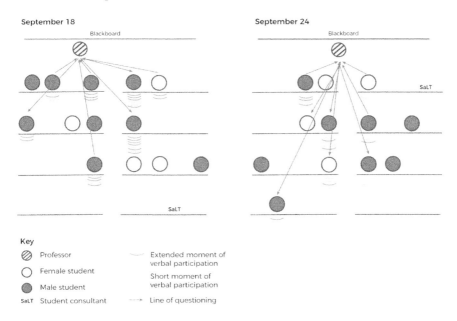

Key

⊘ Professor

◯ Female student

● Male student

SaLT Student consultant

〜 Extended moment of verbal participation

‒ Short moment of verbal participation

⤍ Line of questioning

We see two class sessions in the maps above. The map on the left is early in the semester as students are beginning to establish patterns of speaking. On the right is the following week after Desika asked students to "sit on a different side and in a different row" from where they generally sat. While the total number of students speaking only increased by one, the number of female students speaking increased threefold and the range of students speaking shifted considerably. Desika invited a diverse set of new voices to fill the metaphorical spaces by asking students to shift the physical spaces they occupied in the classroom. Students continued to shift around the classroom in the following weeks. While this movement didn't entirely "solve" the issue of equity in class participation, it did noticeably shift the culture of the class.

Reassuring and Acknowledging

Sophia: I had a lot of anxiety coming into the partnership around working with an astrophysicist because I'd had such negative physics experiences in the past. In prior experiences, the field seemed filled with memorization of complex equations that I could never keep straight. I harbored an assumption that physicists were naturally good at their subject, immediately understanding this new language and easily grasping the importance of topics I struggled with. Embedded in this assumption was the idea that a physicist would be too distanced from my experience of the subject to empathize with what made it difficult. As a woman who did not see herself reflected in her male teachers and professors in physics and complex math, this fear was compounded.

I tried not to let that bias interfere with our work together, but my anxiety was quickly eased. As soon as Desika started by framing the class with the words "We're going to start with what I think is going to be a harder part" and acknowledging the anxiety that might accompany that challenge, I knew this space would feel different.

Desika: I have never been particularly good at physics, astronomy, or math compared to my peers as both a physics major in college and in my astronomy PhD program. I vividly remember being confused about a lecture, going into the next lecture, which started where we left off, which meant I was starting from a place of having no idea what was going on. This was true in both undergraduate and graduate school, which only served to feed my imposter syndrome (a syndrome that, while widespread, particularly impacts minorities in a given field of study; see Lindemann, Britton, and Zundl 2016; Ramsey and Brown 2017). This was something I was (and continue to be) keen on mitigating for students. Identifying topics that are weak links in the overall narrative that might make understanding difficult for students was a primary goal of mine in the student-teacher partnership. This was particularly challenging in the derivation-heavy courses that Sophia and I partnered in, and it was an area where having a student such as Sophia pay attention to the overall flow of a given class was particularly useful.

At the same time, when reflecting on my own insecurities from my experience with STEM courses as an undergraduate student and talking with Sophia about her self-identified anxiety in physics, I wanted students to feel as though I "got" that it was hard. One of the most frustrating aspects of my own education was being taught by professors who didn't understand why I didn't get it. Throughout a lecture, Sophia and I would try to identify areas that we knew would be sticking points and be transparent with the students about that aspect of the lecture. Similarly, recalling areas that I found tricky as an undergraduate in the same course and sharing that with the students was a pedagogical strategy that Sophia and I were able to identify as successful in preventing students from "checking out" when a hard topic arose.

Sophia and Desika: Our shared anxieties helped us focus in our partnership on trying to help students feel welcome in a space that may not have traditionally welcomed them. Desika's intentionality in this area helped to create a close community in the classroom. In the example below, he makes a point of reassuring a student who isn't sure about asking a question. In this instance, he makes sure students know this is a place where asking questions is not only acceptable but encouraged:

Observation	Commentary
10:39 – A student who usually doesn't speak up in class asks a question. He starts by saying, "Sorry" and you say, "No, don't be sorry!"	Thank you for both noticing this and responding–you reinforced, to me, your commitment to answering student questions regardless of where you are in the lecture.

While Desika was able to reassure students that making mistakes is part of the learning process, Sophia was able to reassure him that his own mistakes in class—missing a step when modeling a derivation or forgetting to mention a concept—was a part of teaching and being in a learning community.

Students appreciated when you corrected yourself and/or accepted students' corrections/feedback in class. One noted that when you went over equations and explained where you made a mistake, he learned where one might become confused and was able to not fall into that same trap. Other students appreciated your honesty and that you didn't seem to "need to be right" all the time. They noted that made you more approachable and it was therefore easier for them to ask questions or speak up about their confusion.

Desika had been worried that if he miswrote something or made a small mistake while deriving an equation in class, students would find it confusing and potentially frustrating. Instead, we found, and Sophia was able to share, that this made space for students to more deeply understand and created a community in which mistakes happen and can be fixed.

Building Inclusion through Participation and Community

We came into this partnership informed by our shared experiences of not always feeling comfortable in STEM classrooms. Sophia is a woman who thought maybe she "just wasn't a math person," and Desika faced stumbling blocks in classes where the professor seemed to think this should come easily and naturally. Our partnership allowed us to focus on not reproducing those same feelings of discomfort for any of the students in the class, but most especially for the women and students of color in the class who don't often see successful examples of themselves in physics classrooms.

Our process wasn't particularly scientific. We experimented with many small efforts to build community: using students' names regularly, asking students to move around and meet new peers, frequently changing how students were grouped and encouraging productive group dynamics, encouraging the development of study groups outside of class, regularly checking in with students for feedback, and asking struggling students to meet one-on-one. Women and students of color were underrepresented in both of the semesters we partnered together, but we were thrilled to see that many continued in the field following their experiences in these classes.

As an example, in the fall class we taught, we had a *100% retention rate* into the subsequent spring semester course. This course had twelve students, of whom four identified as women and five were people of color (totaling seven underrepresented minority students, accounting for intersectionality). Of those twelve students, seven have gone on to graduate school in a STEM field, and of those, four are underrepresented minorities. These are nearly identical statistics—58% of the students enrolled were underrepresented minorities, while 57% of the students who went to graduate school were underrepresented minorities. Given the "leaky pipeline" in STEM fields (a phenomenon in which a regular fraction of women and students of color leave the field at every juncture, for example from undergraduate school to graduate school or graduate school to postdoc; see Dubois-Shaik and Fusulier 2015; Flaherty 2018), even maintaining constant numbers is a success. We attribute much of this success to the various techniques that we employed to increase clarity and energy. A beneficial consequence of these techniques was the increased participation and broader empowerment in the sciences of underrepresented minorities. While this is a small sample in formal terms, it's huge for those four students who were so inspired in that first class they decided to make this their disciplinary home.

Final Reflection

Sophia: Our partnership was one of hope and joy. I still remember a particular class in which Desika discussed black hole formation, and while I'm not a physicist by any means, I'm far more comfortable and enthusiastic now being a casual consumer of scientific research and work. Finally, I'm inspired by the many ways Desika opened his process up to examination and change, and I often give examples drawn from this partnership in my work with other faculty.

Desika: I view this partnership as simply transformative for my pedagogical style. I grew up in large university systems (and continue to teach in one) where the style was often combative between students and professors. This partnership taught me how to approach lectures with particular care toward increasing clarity and energy, which has the effect of deepening the in-class relationship between me and the students. At the same time, I have been encouraged by the efficacy of these methods in broadening participation and retention of underrepresented minorities in the field. The viewpoints provided by a student partner in the room, which generated both "general feeling/energy," as well as quantitative evidence of the impact of different pedagogical techniques, were critical to shaping my view of the student-professor relationship in the classroom.

Reflection Questions for Readers

- How can small moments instill a sense of belonging in the classroom and in a partnership?
- What factors have affected your sense of belonging in higher education? What steps can you take (from your position) to positively instill that sense of belonging in others?
- How have classroom activities affected your sense of enthusiasm in a class?

References

Dubois-Shaik, Farah, and Bernard Fusulier. 2015. "Academic Careers and Gender Inequality: Leaky Pipeline and Interrelated Phenomena in Seven European Countries." *GARCIA Working Papers* 5. Trento, Italy: University of Trento. https://eige.europa.eu/sites/default/files/garcia_working_paper_5_academic_careers_gender_inequality.pdf.

Flaherty, Kevin. 2018. "The Leaky Pipeline for Postdocs: A Study of the Time between Receiving a PhD and Securing a Faculty Job for Male and Female Astronomers." (white paper). https://arxiv.org/abs/1810.01511.

Lindemann, Danielle, Dana Britton, and Elaine Zundl. 2016. "'I Don't Know Why They Make It So Hard Here': Institutional Factors and Undergraduate Women's STEM Participation." *International Journal of Gender, Science and Technology* 8 (2): 221-241. http://genderandset. open.ac.uk/index.php/genderandset/article/view/435/791.

Museus, Samuel D., Robert T. Palmer, Ryan J. Davis, and Dina C. Maramba. 2011. "Racial and Ethnic Minority Students' Success in STEM Education." *ASHE Higher Education Report* 36 (6). https://doi. org/10.1002/aehe.3606.

National Academies of Sciences, Engineering, and Medicine. 2016. "The Culture of Undergraduate STEM Education." In *Barriers and Opportunities for 2-Year and 4-Year STEM Degrees: Systemic Change to Support Diverse Student Pathways,* edited by Shirley Malcom and Michael Feder. Washington, DC: The National Academies Press. https://doi.org/10.17226/21739.

Ramsey, Elizabeth, and Deana Brown. 2017. "Feeling Like a Fraud: Helping Students Renegotiate their Academic Identities." *College & Undergraduate Libraries* 25 (1): 86-90. https://doi.org/10.1080/10691 316.2017.1364080.

CHAPTER 13

Personal Growth through Traditional and Radical Partnerships

Anita Ntem
Special advisor to the CEO
Democracy Prep Public Schools
United States

Given my initial lack of knowledge in the field of partnerships, the ambiguity and uncertainty of my role throughout my partnerships fostered several different key opportunities for challenging traditional pedagogy. I exercised patience and strove to fully understand the context of a situation. This essay explores my experience in three distinct partnerships. My first partnership inspired me to learn about the contextual factors that play a role in classroom pedagogy. My second partnership pushed me to accept my discomfort with ambiguity. And my last partnership encouraged me to explore what kind of leader I was becoming. These three partnerships crafted my role and understanding of what it meant to be an effective and meaningful student partner.

The Power of Affirmations: Understanding Contextual Factors in Partnership

During the second year of my undergraduate career, the director of the Students as Learners and Teachers program, Alison Cook-Sather, invited me to participate in a partnership with a faculty member who co-taught a course as part of an immersive, cluster experience. This partnership presented my first moments of uncertainty and helped me understand the importance of learning the full context of a situation and the effects it has on classroom pedagogy. I joined the partnership thinking to myself, *what will I be doing or bringing to this partnership?* I knew that I would be taking notes and observing the professor's class, but I was not entirely sure about how useful I would be. I felt nervous and uncertain. Then, I thought to myself that perhaps all I could do is be a "problem solver." This meant that if my faculty partner informed me of a problem, we would work through the problem together. Yet, when I remembered that my faculty partner had many years of teaching experience, I questioned my effectiveness in troubleshooting any possible issues that would arise.

After my first meeting with my faculty partner, I realized how challenging my role would be. I had to be present in a course that was co-taught by another professor, and I quickly learned that any such co-teaching is always situated in a complex institutional dynamic. I needed to think through how I could provide support for my faculty partner and create a connection with the students. But beyond that, part of growing in this role was understanding that I had to be a malleable person who wore many hats. I made suggestions on how to improve connections with her class, including inviting opinions on ice breakers, taking ownership of team bonding activities, and creating space for whole group reflections. And I also became the support system any time students needed a space to process the complexity of the program. When participating in partnership, it is not always ideal to be an active student in the class and a student consultant simultaneously, because the lines of the roles can be blurred. Being in both roles felt exciting yet exhausting! I reflected on the amount of time, energy, and work students are accountable for outside of class, and it motivated me to be a supporter of both my partner and the students of the course. The dynamics of this partnership propelled me to make sure everyone felt secure, and I did this by ensuring both student and staff confidentiality. I wanted to build and sustain trust with my faculty partner and her students.

When my faculty partner and I met, she opened up to me. She spoke to me about herself, her working relationship with the students, as well as the institutional dynamics within which the course unfolded. It was in this intimate moment that I realized that what she needed most were affirmations. She could not share her thoughts about the realities and limitations of institutional work if she did not feel comfortable. However, understanding these contextual elements affected the way that I reflected on aspects of her pedagogy that I might not have paid attention to during the start of our partnership. Quite frankly, this conversation opened my eyes to not take everything I observed at face value but to always consider the external influences on a decision that is made by a faculty member. I had already admired her sense of confidence in the way that she carried herself, the way she demonstrated respect through her body language, and the way she was able to create a harmonious relationship with her co-teacher. When I saw her vulnerability, there was a shift in my initial assumptions. It became apparent how easy it could be to fall into a mode of self-deprecation and self-judgments when caught up in the technicality of institutional expectations. I felt that she needed acknowledgment and recognition of the impact she had on all her students.

At first, as a student, I did not think professors needed affirmation as much as students. This partnership taught me to think differently. When I expressed my true admiration for how she provided a space for her students to take the initiative, and how her confidence made students feel assured in themselves, she was astonished. She knew she was a great professor, but she did not realize how impactful she was in her relationships with her students and the particular strengths she brought to her pedagogy. Even in my role as a participating student, I felt motivated and energized to continue this academic work. I wanted her to be aware of her strengths, so I made sure to share how her students appreciated her presence, her body language, and the balance she brought to her co-instructional partnership. As Cook-Sather notes: "The student consultant is uniquely positioned as neither student in nor a teacher of the class, yet still a student and focused on supporting the teaching" (2015, 15). My unique position as a student consultant provided me the opportunity to support my faculty partner's teaching, both directly and indirectly. Being able to name the things that students appreciated (and what I appreciated as a student myself) positively reinforced what my faculty partner was already doing well and what she should continue to do. She is an autonomy-supportive professor (Jang, Reeve, and Deci 2010) who creates a warm and welcoming space by encouraging students to finish their sentences before she comments and allows students to take the initiative and ownership of the course materials by allowing students to create content and lead team sessions for the day. She fostered moments of reassurance students could rely on. Had my faculty partner not expressed her own feelings of vulnerability and uncertainty, I would not have known how important it was to affirm her strengths in the class.

Accepting Discomfort and Ambiguity

I brought the growing skill of seeking contextual understanding into my second partnership. I understood that since my partner was a new faculty member, there were many challenges to her feeling welcome and secure in her role. When we first met, I was delighted to learn about how she fell in love with her subject matter and what her goals for the course were. In the first few weeks of our partnership, my method was to acknowledge all the things that seemed to be working well for students, then, if need be, to provide constructive feedback on what needed more attention. However, after the first few weekly check-ins, my faculty partner did not seem as receptive to receiving my feedback as I thought she would be. I experienced what felt to me like resistance and apathy (Ntem and Cook-Sather 2018). I started to feel as though she didn't value my feedback as much because there were more affirmations than constructive criticism. This was reflected in the decrease of our weekly check-ins, her body language, which seemed guarded, and her tone, which displayed moments of inattentiveness. This feeling was unsettling and, from my perspective, decreased the overall consistency of our communication. I felt as though we were not on the same page—like she did not see the benefit of my being physically present in the classroom. During my weekly meetings with other student consultants, which provided us with a space for active reflections and brainstorming action steps for partner work, I shared with the group that my partner did not seem as responsive or receptive to my contributions as she had seemed to be in the very beginning. At that moment, I was not only confused, but I also started to question whether this partnership was worth the time and energy.

During this time, I focused on just thinking through this situation with my fellow cohort of student consultants and weighing the possibilities and ways to move forward. Having a group that was supportive and there for me to help me sort through the ambiguity of partnership was useful (Cook-Sather 2015). One thing I learned from that experience was not only to be patient in not knowing what was next but also to understand that everyone has their own timing and needs space to decipher their own emotions. Not everyone is ready to be fully committed to being in partnership, so I should not take the outcome personally or be self-critical when things do not go as planned.

When my faculty partner was ready to be in communication with me again, we had an honest conversation about ways we could move forward. Part of the process of moving forward was being honest about how we could both be productive in our partnership. We ended up deciding it would be most useful for us to focus on her upcoming course for the next semester.

In this partnership, for us to move forward and maximize productivity, we took a step back to think through what made the most sense to focus our energy on. We agreed to disagree on her approach to fostering student-faculty relationships. This experience of not knowing what to do because of the lack of communication between me and my faculty partner was when I felt almost useless. These feelings have also been shared by other student partners about their partnerships. When my faculty partner and I reconnected, I felt that we started to work toward a common goal, and there was a shift in attitude and approach. We were not perfect by any means, but we were productive in reaching a point of consensus to move forward.

Co-creational Partnership: Becoming a Leader

I carried the lessons I learned from my previous partnerships with me as I approached my last partnership. Acknowledging contextual factors and learning to be okay with not always knowing what was ahead was and still is critical in making the most out of partnership. During my last semester as a student consultant, Alison invited me to participate in an immersive, co-teaching experience with a visiting professor. This experience was excitingly different from my other partnerships because my role evolved as the partnership unfolded. In this partnership, because of our schedules, my faculty partner and I did not have the opportunity to meet in person to fully discuss classroom structures and dynamics before the beginning of the semester. When we finally met after I had the opportunity to sit and observe the course, we had to learn to trust that things would be clearer once we followed the flow of the course.

Not only did we get to know more about each other's lives, but we also had the opportunity to learn about how we each felt about classroom spaces and students' presence. We found that we shared similarities in our ability to deeply reflect on pedagogy and learning spaces. Part of being fruitful in partnership was learning about our differing backgrounds and why we were so passionate about particular elements that shaped learning spaces. When my faculty partner and I thought about how our partnership would be defined for the rest of the semester, we didn't really know what made the most sense. We had a lot of questions regarding what might be most effective. Should my faculty partner teach the first half of the class and I teach the second half? Or should I just take notes on the class dynamics and share feedback with her? I thought to myself that I could also teach a few classes and she could help fill in the gaps. Another alternative that came to mind was continuing to participate in the class half the time and the other half I could take notes. All the emotions of uncertainty about my role were exciting, and clarity started to emerge when we started to have more frequent check-ins.

The possibilities of my new role were endless, which made it bittersweet. I knew that I had the opportunity to try out an abundance of innovative strategies; at the same time, due to the natural time constraints of the course, I had to be strategic about how to optimize my time. We came to the conclusion that I should be in the class and use personal judgment to make appropriate contributions to class content, activities, and discussions. My faculty partner trusted my judgment and initiative, which made me feel honored and excited to work with her. I would feel free to bring up common themes and issues that I noticed in class, and we would clarify and discuss them. I really appreciated how open and flexible she was in figuring out what made sense for us. This flexibility motivated me to have faith in not always having a clear answer but engaging deeply with the process of co-creation.

As our partnership developed, we learned a lot about each other regarding our pedagogical style, personal values, and goals. As a student consultant, I had never had a partnership in which my partner gave me advice and tried to support me in my academic goals. Instead of only advocating for my partner, I also felt advocated for. There were moments where she would remind me that I did not need to take on so many roles. Of course, given who I am, I would say, "No, it is totally fine, really." If I said I was going to do something, I wanted to make sure that I would do it and do it well. I appreciated my role in asking questions, challenging assumptions, and facilitating conversations. I really appreciated that she was always so caring and wanted me to make the most of my experiences by not overworking myself. This partnership brought me a sense of agency and encouraged me to carefully consider what decisions made the most sense. The ability to share my honest feedback on how to encourage students to get out of their comfort zone was priceless.

Looking at my personal growth from my first to last partnerships, I noticed that I always had some form of nervousness and uncertainty, but most importantly, I needed to acknowledge the realities that surrounded the present circumstances. These themes of uncertainty were a motivating factor for me to think thoroughly about what role I wanted to play and the expectations I developed for myself and for the partnership. The moments of uncertainty allowed me to understand what it means to be patient and come to terms with the fact that not everyone will always be ready to be in a fully, committed partnership. Moments of uncertainty gave me a better understanding of contextual factors and afforded me the opportunity to be a leader who recognizes these barriers. I learned to make the most out of a situation and leverage moments of ambiguity as spaces for deep reflection. My last partnership, where I co-taught with my faculty partner, really showed me my growth and maturity. This was a moment when I was seen in a different role. I was one of the holders of subject knowledge. Students trusted me to clarify, explain, and open up. All the moments of uncertainty, misunderstanding, and confusion, as well as careful attention, patience, and readjustment, had led to this moment of leadership. These were the moments I carried with me as I went on to conferences, workshops, and panels discussing the work and energy of what it felt like and meant to be in partnership.

Reflection Questions for Readers

- Must you experience some form of resistance to truly understand the value of partnership?
- Can you fully understand what it means to foster "productiveness" in partnerships when your role in partnership is ambiguous and uncertain?
- What are the ways you can encourage the same effects of agency and empowerment in partnership when you have a partner who is not receptive to your partnership practice?

References

Cook-Sather, Alison. 2015. "Dialogue across Differences of Position, Perspective, and Identity: Reflective Practice in/on a Student-Faculty Pedagogical Partnership Program." *Teachers College Record* 117 (2). http://repository.brynmawr.edu/edu_pubs/32/.

Jang, Hyungshim, Johnmarshall Reeve, and Edward L. Deci. 2010. "Engaging Students in Learning Activities: It Is Not Autonomy Support or Structure but Autonomy Support and Structure." *Journal of Educational Psychology* 102, no. 3 (August): 588-600. http://dx.doi.org/10.1037/a0019682.

Ntem, Anita, and Alison Cook-Sather. 2018. "Resistances and Resiliencies in Student-Faculty Pedagogical Partnership." *International Journal for Students as Partners* 2 (1): 82-96. https://doi.org/10.15173/ijsap.v2i1.3372.

CHAPTER 14

"I've Seen You"

*A Conversation about the Transformative Potential
of Working in Partnership*

Jennifer Fraser
University dir. of student partnership
University of Westminster
United Kingdom

Moonisah Usman
Student partnership prog. coordinator
University of Westminster
United Kingdom

Kate Carruthers Thomas
Senior research fellow
Birmingham City University
United Kingdom

Mayed Ahmed
Undergraduate student
University of Westminster
United Kingdom

Anna Dolidze
Undergraduate student
University of Westminster
United Kingdom

Fathimath Zuruwath Zareer
Undergraduate student
University of Westminster
United Kingdom

Rumy Begum
Senior lecturer
University of Westminster
United Kingdom

Bradley Elliott
Lecturer
University of Westminster
United Kingdom

Evgeniya Macleod
Lecturer
University of Westminster
United Kingdom

bell hooks makes a powerful case for learning in partnership and the potential it contains: "Learning and talking together, we break with the notion that our experience of gaining knowledge is private, individualistic, and competitive. By choosing and fostering dialogue, we engage mutually in a learning partnership" (2010, 43). We also know from anecdotal and published evidence that partnerships can transform student and staff experiences of higher education (Cook-Sather, Bovill, and Felten 2014; Cook-Sather and Luz 2015; Healey, Flint, and Harrington 2014; Peseta et al. 2016).

But what is it about these relationships that is transformative? What factors make successful partnerships? And do partnerships need to be successful to be transformative? These are questions we are asking in a research project on the Students as Co-Creators program at the University of Westminster. Part of our method is to work collaboratively with program participants to create knowledge from within our community.

Our program team has been taking steps over the last year to ensure the program itself is co-created by participants, so everyone has a stake in the program's structures and design. For example, during the summer of 2018, we hosted a series of discussions. Some of these conversations led to the Westminster Co-Creators Principles, an iterative set of principles which outline the type of work that each group aspires toward and commits to on applying to the program. We also spent an afternoon in May with student and staff partners conversing about their experiences of the program and the processes involved in building partnerships. We captured the discussion by audio recording to enable a rich mix of voices and experiences to come through. That conversation and accompanying illustrations is the focus of this chapter.

We chose conversational methods to enact hooks' argument that dialogue can facilitate learning partnerships and applied them to a discussion about the program itself. We wanted to converse across subject positions and disciplines, to create space for reflection and to learn from each another. In the busyness of university life with its pressures to achieve grades, publish, and attend classes and meetings, we do not have many opportunities to pause and converse. This is compounded by pressures for programs to be outcome-driven with measurable impacts. We are attempting to push back against these pressures to consider and prioritize process, particularly the processes of relationship building that are at the heart of student-staff partnerships. To do this, we focussed on being present with one another, thinking out loud, and seeing what emerged. We wanted to foster a generative space with students and staff who were active in the program but who were not necessarily steeped in partnership literature. We hoped to center the lived experiences of partnership as a basis for generating new critical and theoretical approaches. What follows is a narrative approach to demonstrate how the conversation unfolded and how our collective thinking developed. It ends with a series of questions for readers to consider in building their partnerships or programs.

One afternoon in late May after the exam season had finished, we gathered for our conversation. We provided a brief list of guiding questions before the session, but we encouraged everyone not to prepare their answers in advance to allow a conversation to emerge. We had three students: Anna, Mayed, and Zuruwath. Anna and Mayed had each completed multiple projects, while Zuruwath had just completed her first. We also had three members of staff: Rumy, Evgeniya, and Bradley, all of whom had participated in multiple projects. Jennifer and Moonisah, who are responsible for the program, were part of the conversation as well. Finally, we were joined by Kate from Birmingham City University, who illustrated our afternoon.

As we gathered in the room with relatively comfortable furniture and warm drinks, a spectacular summer thunderstorm raged outside. The thunderstorm dramatically punctuated and sometimes paused the conversation. Nonetheless, positive energy filled the room as we listened to each other's accounts of joy, frustration, and learning in partnership.

We began by describing our experiences of the program.

Anna: In one word: "unforgettable." As a final-year student, I'm reflecting, and I keep going back to that first project. Unforgettable because it was a really safe introduction to university life, but it also taught me a lot about employability. It was the reason I got my first job.

Mayed: Unforgettable and exciting. I made lots of friends during the projects. It improved my writing and communication skills. In the last three years doing the projects, I met lots of academics, and they know me now. They say, "Hello." This is actually really exciting. So yeah, I'm proud.

Rumy: I like working with students quite closely. It's more relaxed. Here it's different. I came to a gathering and I met students who were in my faculty. Speaking to them about their ideas and just listening was nice. Then to work together on their idea was so nice. At first, they didn't know what the relationship was. "There's the academic. Does she tell us what to do?" But we found our way.

As the conversation warmed up, we considered the ingredients for successful partnerships.

Anna Dolidze

Bradley: You need buy-in from both partners, and enthusiasm.

Rumy: You can buy in, but you also need the drive to keep it going. It comes at the busiest times, and it's an addition. You do it because you want to, but if there's no person driving it, whether it be students or staff, it won't come to fruition. Good communication is massive.

Anna: It's also about the connection between the team. For me, a successful partnership would have people that complement each other's skills and knowledge and experiences and have a mutual aim. It's really nice to see how the whole team works as one. It's like one big machine, and everyone plays an important part, and if you don't have that part, then the machine wouldn't work.

Evgeniya: I don't think we should consider successful partnership just in terms of the project. When projects finish, that's not the end of the transformation. For example, Anna is on her third project with a different academic partner, but we still communicate very often, even without a formal framework. This kind of partnership is still going because we made a connection.

Mayed Ahmed

Mayed: You have to come to an agreement with your partner that you are both going to do this. Commitment is the main thing, and you both have to make time plans. You have to meet up to see how you are progressing. It's better when academics tell me when I'm doing something right, because that motivates us to do more.

Moonisah: If I was to think of successful partnerships as projects that finished with a decent report with some recommendations, then the successful projects were the ones where the academic and the student understood each other's commitments and communicated well.

Bradley: It's a different relationship from supervision. It needs to be a partnership, not just in name. We're supposed to be helping each other. In the first project, I had a student partner who was also my research undergraduate. I was formally in charge of a major part of her degree, and I was informally part of her making the university better. It worked. We got on really well, as a team.

Rumy: I think it's a bit of a journey. It changes with time. At different points in that journey the students might be doing more, and you might be doing more at some points, and that evolves. But your goal is the same: you want to complete that project in a good way so that it can lead to changes.

From here, our conversation shifted a little as we realized that we needed to develop a clearer idea of what we meant by success. We came up with a working definition: in the context of partnership projects, success means that something changes or shifts or is different at the end of the process. As we discussed what this meant, we moved to thinking through what happens in partnerships that don't meet their goals or complete their projects, or when nothing changes.

Evgeniya: In my case, it just takes longer. It's not a failure. It's this realization that a transformation that's needed might happen slowly. You need to look to long-term results, how these practices have been implemented.

Anna: Sometimes there's a danger when you're really busy, both as a student and academic, to put the project aside. If you forget why you started in the first place and what the long-term goal is, then it can be very tricky to get back on track. You need to recognize you're not alone in the team.

Moonisah Usman

Moonisah: Absolutely, and there are some assumptions made. Some staff think, "If the students are not getting in touch with me, that means they're okay and they know what they're doing." But sometimes that's not the case. On the other side, students say, "Is it okay for me to keep emailing my academic partner with all these different questions?" But that's the point of partnership, you should feel comfortable in approaching them when you need to.

Rumy: I think it can be less successful if you're not drip . . . drip . . . drip . . . drip feeding into this project. You need to have quite regular, even if it's little, contact. Whoever it is, that constant little "I'm here. We're doing this" is important.

We also began to unpack what we meant by success, especially in terms of thinking about who or what should change as a result of the projects.

Evgeniya: How do you define success? If I didn't affect two hundred academics in Westminster Business School, but three students transformed their lives, or me and a few friends are inspired to improve our teaching practice, is that success? If I teach and it changes a few people, over the years it will transform into more people.

Bradley: That makes sense. This is supposed to be about making things better. If you have an institutional change, then you're making things better. If you identify something could improve—and the whole point of student direction is that you know better than we do what's going wrong—and we don't make a change then that's not successful. Don't get me wrong, improved confidence, skills, and employability is great, but the aim of the project in my mind was to make Westminster a better place, and if we are not doing that then we're failing. It's a project that's not implementing its goal.

Jennifer Fraser

Jennifer: As you were all talking, I had an image of a pond with a rock that goes in the middle, and then ripples spread outwards. I think projects can be really successful for the participants but not ripple further, but that doesn't mean it's not successful. Or they can have some success in changing the way something happens locally. Others will make a change at a University level, and then people go to conferences or get on social media and actually change things outside the institution. Something might not change inside the institution in terms of policies or structures, but someone else takes hold of the idea and runs with it outside. There are different circles of change.

Bradley Elliott

Bradley: Getting to see an undergraduate student do a presentation at a major conference. There were 150 people in the audience, and they quizzed her afterward. She stood there and held her own. It was really nerve-wracking because it was one of the first times in my career where I thought, "Right, that's your thing. I'm going to stand back and let you take the kudos for it because you did this." It was awesome.

In the conversation, it became clear that almost everyone had been involved in multiple projects. We were curious about what motivated this continued engagement.

Rumy: I like building relationships and finding new people to work with.

Anna: It was my first year, and I was super lost and was thinking, "Oh no, I made a mistake. I came to the UK to do my degree, and now I'm here and I have no idea what I'm doing, I have no friends." I met people, but friendships are not that easy to make unless you spend proper time together like you do as part of a partnership. And when I heard about Co-Creators, I was like, "I should totally do it." And I did. It was horrible at first because it was a very broken team, but we actually created a really nice team. I continued afterward because there were these amazing friendships, and I improved my knowledge of how the University operates.

At this point in the conversation, we shifted away from thinking about success to thinking about how working in partnership can lead to transformations in our learning and teaching. We began to discuss the specific types of changes that have come about through practicing learning to work in partnership.

Rumy Begum

Rumy: I'm not sure if it's this or just generally, but over the last year I've been a bit more active on social media. I take part in a lot of conversations . . . the Learning & Teachings chats on Wednesday evenings. You have students and academics all giving their perspectives, and I quite like that. I think this makes me want to be more part of that and hear from different experiences, from different institutions, from different circles. It makes me more engaged with that type of social media where I can utilize these conversations in my practice as well.

Evgeniya: It's also understanding students much more after this project. I get much better feedback from students and understand how they learn, how they feel, what affects them, and that's all happening because we did that first project. Without the project, we would not have developed a relationship where I could get insight into what students think. That transformation was quite interesting.

Anna: I second that. I was in first year, and after doing the project, I knew what research was—how to conduct it, to write reports, to deliver presentations. I had this really proud moment when I was taught market research and I thought, "Oh yeah, I've done that, I've done both primary and secondary research." It made the learning experience much easier. I've really developed friendships with students and staff and gotten to know myself throughout the years: what I like, what I don't like, what I need to improve, what I'm good at.

Bradley: I gained an understanding of the students from their point of view and how to communicate better with them. It's been a long time since I was a student. In the first year, I would give a lecture and think, "Oh my God, I told you this five times, I told you in your lecture, I wrote it in the handbook, it's on the assessments, on BlackBoard, and you can't find it." I was quite grumpy. I've learned how to communicate more effectively or in different mediums so different people get it.

Evgeniya: Even in my teaching, I tend to be moving towards partnership rather than, "I'm the teacher, the boss, I'm telling you what to read, etc. . . ." It's just naturally different now.

Mayed: I feel more confident. Now I can ask any academic a question and they answer. It definitely built up my relationship skills.

Fathimath Zuruwath Zareer

Anna: From a student perspective, when you do that type of project you inevitably break down the barriers that may exist between staff and students, because you think, "Oh, this is an academic. I shouldn't mess up in front of them or ask something silly." But when you do the partnership you realize it's just another human being and we all make mistakes, we all get super excited about something, or super sad, and we all have burning questions. You get the backstage view of what's going on in the life of an academic. So maybe you understand better why that email didn't come the next day or the same day, but it came after one week. I think it's mutual.

Zuruwath: I became more conscious of things that are happening inside the university. Before it would be things that I had identified as complaints, but after the project, I see these as things that can be improved.

As people shared, we began to consider what it is about the ways of working that emerge in partnership—through the structures of the Co-Creators program and the modes that groups create for themselves—that give them the possibility of being transformative.

Evgeniya: Commitment to dreaming about a better world. If you get a few people together thinking and discussing what would make it better, it's inspiring, you have a dream. I think partnerships make you think, "What can we do to make it better?" There's a commitment to positive thinking because you have a project where you need to meet deadlines, and you have a friendship that continues, and you're still talking about what could make it better.

Evgeniya Macleod

Anna: It's also about safety. From a student perspective, we have a safety net behind us to make mistakes because it's a university environment and we have an academic partner. That's very good preparation for the real world, because when you leave university and you start a job, you can make mistakes, but you will try not to because if you make a mistake, it's a big deal because you are paid for this job. Here you learn from your mistakes and then you do it better next time.

Mayed: It's teamwork and a friend relationship between the academic and the student, so it boosts your confidence to talk about your ideas and develop listening skills which are really important. You have to listen to each other to come up with a better solution.

Rumy: In smaller groups, the transformation is more intense. You get to understand the students, the students get to understand you, and the learning is there from both perspectives. These projects are a bit research-like. When I work with students initially, I try and engage where they're at, and actually they know very little, depending on whatever stage they've come from. For me, the transformation was actually—they didn't know about little things that we take for granted. The transformation was realizing that you can't expect certain things to just happen, you need a lot of input from both angles.

Zuruwath: It's the actual work that we are doing with these partnerships that is transformative; no one comes to Uni thinking they're going to be working alongside the Uni. Everyone imagines academics to be a separate group of which they have a little knowledge. They go to them for advice, but we don't really get opportunities to be on the same level as academics, as the university, and see things from the university's perspective. There is a shift in perspective.

Anna: It's the sense of community and belonging, isn't it?

In the final part of our conversation, we grappled with what space the projects offer for transformation if they are not completing or making change, particularly if they are not making an institutional-level change.

Anna: Success is individual. Even the mistakes build some kind of foundations for future transformation. So next time you're doing this, whether it's this same project outside the university or your personal life, you know what not to do if you make mistakes. If everything went well, then next time you can improve. Inevitably it ends in some kind of transformation, whether or not it's instant or happens after time.

Rumy: These partnerships work not just within your own little community. I could always be stuck in science and technology, but what I find interesting is you're meeting so many individuals at so many different

levels. It may not be beyond this room afterward, but when you see them again, it's just like, "I've seen you."

Our conversation was an opportunity to think through and surface our ideas about success and transformation in the context of student-staff partnership projects. It is not only the content but also the method we used that we think is helpful for others in considering their programs or partnerships, whether it be to create new ones or develop existing ones. Ultimately, it was, as Rumy suggested, an opportunity to *see* one another and engage with one another differently and thus to enrich our collective understandings of partnership.

Reflection Questions for Readers

- What does success mean to the members of your partnerships?
- What methods can you use to foster discussion about success before, during, and after partnerships?
- How is it possible to make space for an emphasis on process over product in your partnerships?
- What methods can you use to ensure that program participants have a stake in the program itself and not just in their individual partnerships?

References

Cook-Sather, Alison, Catherine Bovill, and Peter Felten. 2014. *Engaging Students as Partners in Learning and Teaching: A Guide for Faculty.* San Francisco, CA: Jossey-Bass.

Cook-Sather, Alison, and Alia Luz. 2015. "Greater Engagement in and Responsibility for Learning: What Happens When Students Cross the Threshold of Student–Faculty Partnership." *Higher Education Research & Development* 34 (6): 1097-109. https://doi.org/10.1080/07294360.2014.911263.

Healey, Mick, Abbi Flint, and Kathy Harrington. 2014. *Engagement through Partnership: Students as Partners in Learning and Teaching in Higher Education.* York, UK: Higher Education Academy. https://

www.advance-he.ac.uk/knowledge-hub/engagement-through-partnership-students-partners-learning-and-teaching-higher.

hooks, bell. 2010. *Teaching Critical Thinking: Practical Wisdom.* London, UK: Routledge.

Peseta, Tai, Amani Bell, Amanda Clifford, Annette English, Jananie Janarthana, Chelsea Jones, Matthew Teal, and Jessica Zhang. 2016. "Students as Ambassadors and Researchers of Assessment Renewal: Puzzling Over the Practices of University and Academic Life." *International Journal for Academic Development* 21 (1): 54-66. https://doi.org/10.1080/1360144X.2015.1115406.

CHAPTER 15

Sitting on Rocks, Human Knots, and Other Lessons I Learned in Partnership

Anne Bruder
Associate professor
Berea College
United States

In 2009, during the first few weeks of my postdoctoral fellowship, I ran into two students on the path in front of Bryn Mawr College's library. In the customary way, we stopped and chatted. I casually asked, "So what are you guys into?" I was thinking about those puffy pretzels that had become a staple of my Philadelphia diet. Jen grinned and chirped, "Mostly Marianne Moore's juvenilia." I laughed nervously. She was serious and twenty. Sam looked a bit baffled by the lightness of my question but followed up nonetheless: "Images of Joan of Arc, but really only in French." She was serious too. I was in trouble.

I had arrived at Bryn Mawr thankful to have an academic job but insecure about my identity as a professor. While I had been teaching steadily since I was twenty-two, I had always felt a bit like a character actress, mimicking the role that I had watched as a student for decades: the rigorous interlocutor. The contours of this role are simple. You enter the classroom smiling but serious. You regale the students, your audience, with what appears to be insider knowledge about the material for the day. You prepare a few ingenious formulations, a couple borrowed from a recent article and another from an incisive bit of New Criticism from 1964. You give credit, of course, to these sources, and that, in turn, gives you more credibility with your audience. You seem to have read it all. Then you pivot to the students and begin the "dialogue." Only, you know that it isn't really a dialogue because you have "the answers" and they do not. Nonetheless, you pretend that your increasingly abstruse questions are leading them to some sort of truth that you alone know. All the while, you maintain control.

By the time that I stepped on to that neo-Gothic campus, I had mastered this role. My students, in turn, *liked* me. They gave me rave reviews. Occasionally, it even seemed that they wrote a bit better, and perhaps, even thought a bit more carefully at the end of term. Mostly, though, I think they enjoyed the performance. It didn't ask much of them because they had mastered their own passive role long ago and my sporadic, animated rants kept the room feeling light, fun. We had inside jokes and relished them.

But this outward success masked a more complicated story about what was actually happening in my classroom. I began to doubt that my students grew meaningfully in my courses. I came to believe, in fact, that the work we did together had little resonance for them outside of our shared space. Together we might create what seemed a riveting conversation about a single line in an Emily Dickinson poem, the room pulsing with excited speculation, but then the hour would be over, the students putting away their books. All of that excitement seemed nothing more than a transient glimmer of clarity, a flash in the pan.

There was no reason, I recognized, that Dickinson's poem alone should catalyze students' growth or transformation, but I believed nonetheless that, in the space of the classroom, we could together trouble through her lines and in that struggle, find ways to speak across difference and leverage critique as a way to be better citizens in democracy. I could imagine, in other words, what I wanted my classroom to become, but I had no idea how to get there.

In the midst of this vocational crisis, I was fortunate to enroll in a pedagogy course with Alison Cook-Sather. On the first day of the seminar, Alison initiated seated introductions, but then immediately we were all up at the chalkboard, dust on our hands, having a "silent discussion" or "chalk talk" about learning. Silent board discussions focus on the communal possibilities of writing in the classroom. They also allow students to quietly generate their own perspectives about the topic at hand and then begin to put them in conversation with other students in the class. The instructor identifies a key concept for the day and writes that on the board. She then invites all students to gather near the board and begin to populate it with a written discussion. In my classroom, I enforce total silence during this activity so that all students can "listen" to the conversation unfolding on the board. In many classes, it makes sense to ask all students to contribute to the conversation a particular number of times (3-4 works well). After several minutes, I ask students to pause, step back from the board, absorb what they see happening and then contribute again. Following this activity, I have students write about the process itself or extend some of the thinking in a full paragraph of their own.

I watched as the "conversation" spread across the black plane, feeling both exhilarated and confused. Why was it that this simple gesture of translating spoken discussion to the physical realm of standing, writing, reading, and moving seemed to open up a hungry space in all of us? No one hung back. At one point, I stood on my tiptoes and stretched my arm long to respond to a classmate's claim in the upper right corner. Occasionally, we'd all momentarily retreat and read around the dialogue before we leapt back to the board and scribbled out one more response.

I remember the whole seminar as a series of moments like this one. At each meeting, we moved our bodies, stitching our ideas to physical gestures or bits of quick writing, solidifying in memory new ideas about what was possible in the classroom when we liberate ourselves from its conventions. As a student in this seminar, I had the uneasy sense that I was finally learning something that would adhere in my brain over the long run. I say "uneasy" because this also signified just how much of my previous learning had disappeared. Alison's course woke me up by asking me to be a student once again, and I wanted to provide a similar experience for my own students, but I doubted that I would be able to pull it off as a teacher. I knew that it meant performing a new role in the drama around the seminar table and I wasn't quite sure that I had the chops.

That's where partnership came in. Alison encouraged me to give it a try during the next semester. The Teaching and Learning Institute's (TLI) pedagogical partnership program, Students as Learners and Teachers, provided me the opportunity to work on my teaching with a trained student partner for one semester. She attended my course once each week and provided me detailed observations of my classroom. In turn, we met over coffee each Friday and talked through her feedback.

My first student partner was a Bryn Mawr senior about to graduate that spring. She was confident, organized, and most importantly, experienced in TLI's pedagogical partnership program. I knew that she had previously worked successfully in other partnerships and I immediately trusted her instincts. We agreed that she would begin attending my literature course. I knew the material very well but could not help but feel the same old flatness of the class coupled with a now-familiar sense that every day was another flash in the pan, all of this brought into sharp relief by the dimensionality of Alison's seminar the previous term. The other challenge shaping the course was a Bi-College rift between two student cohorts within in it; a group of Bryn Mawr students populated the right and center of the room, and a small, but no less vocal, group of Haverford women took up their position on the left side of the room. The Bi-College Consortium, or Bi-Co, allows Bryn Mawr and Haverford students to take courses and select majors, amongst other opportunities, at either college. The sides resisted engaging one another. Each group regularly responded to me, but I could not figure out how to get them to communicate across the institutional barrier. I described these challenges to my partner before she came into the class for the first time in the third week of the term. Later, when we sat down to meet about her initial observation, she let me indulge in my self-doubt about how the class was going before coolly diagnosing the problem, and in turn, providing the solution: "You're right. The classroom culture isn't working. You need to do the human knot."

"The human *what?*" I asked, incredulous.

"The human knot. You know, where you all hold hands, get all tangled up, and have to work together to undo the knot without breaking the chain."

I laughed, nervously. I hoped she was kidding.

"You can choose to do it silently or not," she added, as if that stipulation would make the prospect of it any brighter. "Either way, you need to do the knot."

"I'm not doing the human knot. No way." I looked her straight in the eye.

By the next week, I was standing in the middle of our classroom, desks pushed to the sides, my palms sweating into two students' hands. I was doing the human knot. This wasn't the performance that I had practiced for so many years in graduate school. But we were all laughing. Several of the women fell on the floor; there were at least two acrobatic feats of bodily contortion, and this was the closest the cohorts had come to something like a shared dialogue (we had chosen the non-silent option after all). I was part of the knot myself, tangled up in undergraduate bodies and quickly losing all sense that I was supposed to be exerting something like control. Only later did I learn that the human knot is nearly impossible with as many participants as we had, but we persisted nevertheless, and eventually, unwound into a catawampus oval, some of us turned inside out, all of us disheveled and disoriented.

I brought cookies that day, too, and after the unexpected aerobics, we munched on buttery confections and processed the activity. At the time, we were studying early American literacy, and in particular we were looking at hornbooks and the *New England Primer.* Without my guiding them, my students made the leap and began talking about how the human knot seemed like a twenty-first-century model of embodied learning, not wholly dissimilar from the rather foreign seventeenth-century notion of tying a hornbook to one's waist and carrying around the possibility of learning. It seemed a stretch to me, but then, I found myself just listening. I had no agenda because I hadn't imagined the connection. After all, I had taken my partner's advice because I wanted to improve the "classroom culture." Rather naively, I didn't realize that doing so would open up spaces for authentically new ideas to emerge. The human knot, I then realized, wasn't *about* the human knot; it was about changing the rules of the classroom. This made it either my craziest performance in the role of "professor" or, perhaps, the entire performance had ended, and we were all just humans learning together. It was hard to tell.

Whenever I tell colleagues the story of doing the human knot for first time, I'm usually met with blank stares. This inevitably turns into leading *that* group through the activity, a hilarious foray into embodied learning with often-reluctant, late-middle-aged professors. I've been twisted up so many times since that first day that I no longer bristle at the first touch. I shouldn't be surprised, but always am, by how that knot again performs its magic and the group's conversations deepen, reaching new understandings.

I can tell with certainty, though, that the human knot works because it makes learning an embodied practice. It says to students that this is a place in which we all stretch ourselves, in which we rely on one another to pull us in new directions, in which we are all equally twisted up. The human knot, of course, is also a metaphor for collective liberation, as the group patiently works together until every member has been freed. Any individual break sends the whole group back to the beginning. No one can be passive because on the most basic level, every *body* must move, must count, must be part of the solution. The metaphor illuminates a new paradigm for class discussions. If a conversation is dominated by a single student's confusion, I can ask a classmate to "untangle" what she hears him saying. When a student is hanging back and letting his peers do all of the discussion work, with a little prompting, I watch as his classmates work to create spaces for him to move into and through.

When I moved to Berea College in Kentucky, I brought the knot with me, and yet, nearly a decade later and now twenty years into teaching, I was becoming cynical again about what was possible in the space of my classroom. In a world that felt ever more urgent and changing, especially in the era of Donald Trump, my courses had started to seem like antique relics. I even found myself slipping into something like a lecture mode, so impatient had I grown at the pace of most student learning. To make matters worse, I stubbornly persisted in marching my students through tepid essay assignments that rewarded traditional forms of excellence in prose: concision, clarity, consistency. All of these have real value in a world in which written and oral communication is fundamental, of course, but in training my focus on these alone, I was strangling my students, or at least turning them into generic writing machines. Fortunately, I didn't like the professor I had become and I certainly didn't like the way that I justified my behavior. I entered partnership again.

With Alison's advice and guidance, I worked with Leslie Orquist-Ahrens, the director of the Center for Teaching and Learning and the director of faculty development at Berea, to implement a program like Bryn Mawr and Haverford's TLI. We called it Berea College's Student-Faculty Partnership Program. While facilitating the program with Leslie in its first year, I became increasingly aware that I, myself, needed partnership and so I stepped away from my leadership role and became a participant once again.

When Riley Lanham and I first met in January 2018, I told her that I wanted to work on my assignments for a literature course that I was teaching for the second time. I wanted the assignments to matter, to prompt real thinking, to stay with students. But I also told her that I was torn between two conflicting aims: needing my students to be traditionally "effective" writers and wanting them to think creatively, imaginatively, and to solve real problems presented in the texts under consideration. I felt up against a wall. Much like my Bryn Mawr partner had years earlier, Riley generously listened to my concerns and then patiently read through my first essay assignment. With equal measures confidence and polite hesitation, she suggested that she wouldn't really want to do *any* of the options that I gave. When I was honest with myself, I didn't want to either.

What Riley saw immediately, and to which I was unaccountably blind, was that this particular literature—canonical essays by Ralph Waldo Emerson and Henry David Thoreau—practically insisted on more engaging, embodied kinds of learning. Thus, she encouraged me to transform my first assignment from a rather dusty question about theoretical connections between the writers into an experiential project that took students to the woods in an unseasonably cold January to sit and read Thoreau outside. They then had to return indoors, contribute to a digitally crowdsourced reading of *Walden,* and finally, integrate the source text, their physical experience, and their online participation into an exploratory examination of Thoreau's claims in his *Walden* chapter "Sounds." By creating a "course group," my students were able to contribute to the Reader's Thoreau where they annotated "Sounds" and engaged the ongoing discussion of other students and scholars on that chapter. Given the physical demands of the assignment, I told students they could elect to write one of the more conventional prompts if they, for whatever reason, could not do the new option. As luck would have it, about half of the course selected each option. I had unwittingly created a pedagogical experiment.

The results surprised me. Before I opened the assignment files, I anticipated that the students selecting the traditional assignment would score higher and write better because, as college students, they should have had years practicing this kind of project, a thesis-driven analytical essay. But the opposite was true. It was that very familiarity that doomed these essays to being conventional, comparatively trite, constrained by the rigidity of the form itself. The new assignment, on the other hand, opened up unexplored spaces, both in terms of form and in terms of connected thinking. Neither I nor the students had any idea of where the projects would end up, making the learning process more authentic. There was no "right" or "smart" answer lurking behind the prompt. The writing, in turn, was better by leaps and bounds. On average, they scored twenty percent higher than their peers. More importantly, they talked about how difficult the new essay was and also about how much they loved it. And perhaps the most unexpected outcome for a literature professor was that I found myself authentically enjoying their submissions, a pedagogical win for everyone.

This kind of assignment became the norm as the semester unfolded. Riley encouraged me to trust my instincts and integrate my idea of experimental "side hustles" into analytical assignments in the middle of the term. After drafting close-readings essays, students completed projects that extended their thinking beyond analytical prose. For instance, students choosing to write about home-keeping in Henry David Thoreau's *Walden* or Elizabeth Oaks Smith's *Western Captive* built 3D models of imagined, radical twenty-first century homes. Several students created musical playlists to capture a particular character's investment in the natural world and in self-invention; still others collected nineteenth-century images of "savages" and contemporaneous portraits of Native American leaders in a small digital archive and then considered the ways in which visual propaganda both supported and contested expulsion. In these projects, students departed from the relatively safe terrain of the academic essay. In turn, they translated their investment in the literature into a form that was at once unfamiliar and generative.

At the close of the term, with Riley's support, I developed a final exploratory project connecting *Uncle Tom's Cabin* to a local community and its claims of inspiring Harriet Beecher Stowe's novel. Students drove into the hills, combed the county's archives, kept a late-night vigil at an eighteenth-century cemetery, came to class bragging about what they'd turned up, and worked in partnership with their classmates. Following all of these new assignments, it would have felt regressive to give a conventional final exam. So Riley and I built a final "experience" (as opposed to a final "exam") with the explicit goal of making it a place for students to consolidate and extend their semester-long learning. In advance of the exam, they recorded their thinking while on a series of walks and then during the exam, they worked through a series of guided prompts to connect the course's readings to their own concerns and experiences.

Just as the human knot worked because I trusted my first partner's suggestion and ceded control to an unknown outcome, these new assignments worked because I again trusted my partner and decided to move the course into an unknown terrain. Both of my experiences in partnership share this quality: ceding control and leaping into a space with an unpredictable outcome. At a glance, these risks may seem insignificant, but they are no less important for the tone they lend the classroom. With each group, I spoke openly about why I was trying these unusual things. I didn't belabor the point, but I wanted them to see me as someone very much in the mix with them, willing to take chances and grow as a teacher.

This kind of pedagogical transparency, of course, relies on a kind of humility or vulnerability that may, at first, seem at odds with a more traditional, authoritative stance in the classroom. A trusting partnership, though, makes this kind of vulnerability far less unnerving because there is an established relationship in which to process the peaks and valleys of any given event, assignment, or day in the course. More important still is the realization that in ceding a measure of authority, my students, in turn, incline toward authorizing themselves to direct their own learning. When, through partnership, I feel confident enough to loosen the reins of control, I've watched my students become empowered enough to follow their own curiosity and to engage one another in finding answers to their questions and concerns. By disposition, I'm comfortable pivoting in and out of the role as the "expert," but it has been partnership that allowed me to reside all semester long in the stance that believes my students to be the essential creators of their own knowledge and experience.

Reflection Questions for Readers

- As a faculty member, what are your impediments to transparency with your students? How does it *feel* to dwell in a space of experimentation with your students?
- How do external pressures limit your vision of the possible for partnership?
- For student partners: Riley was able to see my material in ways that I overlooked; with what frame of mind do you think she was able to draw the conclusions that she did? How might "reading for class" be different than "reading for partnership"?

CONCLUSIONS/OPENINGS

Things that Make Us Go Hmmm

Lucy Mercer-Mapstone
Lecturer
University of Sydney
Australia

Sophia Abbot
Master's student
Elon University
United States

In our introductory poem defining partnership, the seventh stanza focused on the questions that push us to "stretch ourselves / in which we rely on one another to pull us in new directions, / in which we are all equally twisted up" drawn from Anne Bruder's words in chapter 15. Each of our chapters has ended with a collection of questions that has asked you, our readers, to do just that. Across chapters, our authors have explored the complex, messy, challenging, and wonderful intersections between partnership and our world. They have asked questions that aim to get at the heart of: How do we partner? How do we push on power? How do we facilitate equity, inclusion, belonging, community . . . ? How do we make space for ourselves to learn, to represent, and to be represented? How do we reimagine what exists? These are wide and deep questions, and we hope this book has begun to answer as well as complicate them. We hope this book has helped you find ways to think anew.

There are important implications that have arisen in these chapters. When we tried to split them as they applied to various groups (students, staff, administrators), we happily found that virtually all of our conclusions were appropriate for all readers. We think this says something about this collection and about partnership more broadly: while differences are important in the way we come together to create a stronger whole, partnership has the power to position us all as *learners*.

Partners as Allies and Advocates

Chapters 7 (Matthews), 10 (Mathrani and Cook-Sather), 11 (Flint), and 15 (Bruder) in particular helped us see the deep value and power in student experiences, in and of themselves. We are reminded that each of us has particular access to places and knowledges that our partners do not. Students have particular access to understanding other students—for example, in chapter 10 where students are more able to tap into honest, meaningful, and deep feedback on teaching from other students. Staff sometimes have more leverage with other staff, as in chapter 2 (Wilson et al.) where staff hold more legitimacy in inaccessible places where students historically do not "belong" like conferences. Partners act as bridges or conduits—making these places more accessible for those traditionally excluded, sharing that burden of justification (chapter 2, Wilson et al.). Partners can see this as a source of empowerment and should grow confident in their experiential expertise. In doing so, partners may need to become advocates for each other. This notion was explored in chapter 1 in the context of faculty needing to advocate for students in broader academic spaces, and further emerged in chapter 9 (Guitman and Marquis) in the context of students advocating for their faculty partners who may hold marginalized identities within higher education (i.e., women, people of color, LGBT, etc.). Through these chapters, we see this mutual support and ally-ship as not only being possible, but imperative.

Diverging from Traditional Texts

From the beginning, we suspected that diverse genres were needed to capture the nuances and messiness of partnership. Our authors confirmed this and played with genre—challenging the traditions of academic texts. Chapter 11 (Flint) is perhaps the most radical of chapters in sharing experiences (personal, evidenced, and anecdotal) through poetry. Chapter 5 (Lenihan-Ikin et al.) did the same. Chapters 7 (Matthews), 8 (Bell, Barahona, and Stanway), 10 (Mathrani and Cook-Sather), and 14 (Fraser et al.) skipped the text-only approach altogether and integrated incredible illustrations to transform how we engage with their ideas. As editors, we felt a deep connection with every chapter as authors communicated partnership in ways that made the intangible concrete and the messiness clear. We rarely experience this in more traditional academic articles. As Abbi Flint (chapter 11) says: "Poetry itself can be a form of partnership, a dialogue between poet and reader." Indeed, multiple chapters integrated a dialogue among the authors in ways that centered dialogue as core to partnership and invited readers into the conversation more deeply. We feel this applies to all of the diverse genres here—that the bucking of tradition reflects what happens in partnership. The success of these chapters reinforces our argument that alternative genres are appropriate and sometimes necessary for sharing the realities of partnership work.

Centering Power for Ongoing Discussion

Chapter 5 (Lenihan-Ikin et al.) recognizes the reality of the world in which we work, and reminds us:

> A partnership project does not have to ensure *equality* between student and staff partners: that is unachievable (students do not have offices to host meetings in, academics do; students do not always get paid, academics do; research is not always a requirement of undergraduate study, but it is required of academics). Students as partners processes can, however, be *equitable.* This requires deliberate recognition of voice, identity, power, and privilege by all parties.

This differentiation between equality and equity in partnership is a critical one. Aiming for an unrealistic equality in power may risk taking critical conversations about power differentials off the table; if we pretend power can be made equal or has ceased to impact our work, we silence those who are marginalized even more (Eddo-Lodge 2017). Our collection tells us that power isn't going anywhere and perhaps needs even more explicit attention than we currently give it—particularly at the intersection between individual power and privilege, and structural power and privilege. Let's dive in and get comfortable with being uncomfortable as we dig into questions like: how do structural systems of power and oppression like racism or sexism play out in and impact our partnerships and our discussions about power in partnership? Rather than higher education being "the great equalizer," current systems are actually more likely to amplify differences (Carnevale and Strohl 2013). Instead of erasing our *selves* from our work, partnership calls us to be embodied—embracing our diverse genders, races, ethnicities, and identities. In this way, as Anne articulates in chapter 15, partnership becomes a human knot: "No one can be passive because on the most basic level, every body must move, must count, must be part of the solution."

When we bring our true selves to partnership, then, we must reflect on what histories we bring to our relationships. Chapter 1 (Verwoord and Smith) offers us a timely framework through which we can reflect on our partnerships in this way—explicitly surfacing tensions for thoughtful and reflective discussion. We urge readers not to shy away from these discussions because they are too uncomfortable or awkward or because we don't know how to bring them up. Use the P.O.W.E.R. framework and the other resources shared in this collection to consider the ways in which power asymmetries at individual and structural levels influence our partnerships in ways that hold great potential to either oppress or liberate. As Rachel and Beth emphasize in chapter 9, these constant discussions are particularly important in current times as, in a political and social era in which division is quickly becoming an assumed norm, partnership has the power to connect and progress us.

"Difficult" Emotions Belong Here

Previous work has highlighted the importance but frequent omission of emotions from partnership work (Felten 2017; Hermsen et al. 2017). While it is important to celebrate the joy in this work—and we see a lot of joy in the pages of this collection—it is just as important to acknowledge and learn from the troubling or difficult emotions that surface in partnership, of which there can be many given the complex nature of the work. Chapter 12 (Narayanan and Abbot), for example, highlights the power of shared anxiety within and outside partnership contexts as a potential liberation when explicitly acknowledged by all involved:

"Our shared anxieties helped us focus in our partnership on trying to help students feel welcome in a space that may not have traditionally welcomed them." This reminds us that partnerships, unlike traditional university spaces which demand detachment, are a space where emotions can be surfaced and valued—even (or especially) the difficult ones.

Partnership as a House of Mirrors

Reflect, reflect, reflect. Reading through these pages can feel a bit like wandering through a house of mirrors: authors gaze at their own reflections and peer at how they are reflected in the work of others; readers see themselves reflected in the pages. And more often than not, those reflections are distorted in the pleasurable and disconcerting ways typical of a house of mirrors. The common thread throughout, though, is that reflection is a foundation of partnership.

An echoing call is thus made in this collection for both personal and collaborative reflection at every stage of the partnership process. Chapter 10 (Mathrani and Cook-Sather) pushes us to be open to the non-linear, rhizomatic ways in which we grow through partnership. Sasha and Alison reiterate that reflection is that which makes such invisible growth visible, helping us to fully grasp our own growth over time. Chapter 14 (Fraser et al.) makes a similar call—arguing and enacting the value of dialogic spaces for reflecting collectively on partnership as a method of learning from one another by centering "the lived experiences of partnership." Anita Ntem, in chapter 13, shares her own reflections on partnership—bringing the reader into her journey navigating multiple partnerships to becoming more fully and powerfully herself. How do you see yourself reflected in these pages?

Problematising Partnership "Projects"

Chapters 11 (Flint), 14 (Fraster et al.), and 15 (Bruder) all discuss the ways that different partnerships—with different people or over different contexts or times—have accelerated, scaffolded, and reinforced personal growth and learning. These messages hold important implications for how institutions conceptualize the structuring and scaling of partnership. It is increasingly common for institutions to implement student-staff partnership programs or schemes as a method of scaling up partnership. These schemes appear to predominantly adopt a "project-based model of partnership" where each partnership is seen and administered as a distinct project (Mercer-Mapstone and Bovill 2019). Indeed, many of our authors discuss their "partnership projects." This model has various advantages—chapter 14 (Fraser et al.) describes a very successful model of project-based partnership—but it also comes with limitations.

If partnership is seen as restricted to a distinct project, what does that say about the confinement of the partnership mindset (as described by Peseta et al. in chapter 6) to that single context? With a project-based language, are we preventing ourselves from fully incorporating that mindset into our way of being? Limiting the learning opportunities afforded when applied outside that singular context? Projects are a familiar language and structure in institutions, and it makes sense we revert to the familiar when developing something new. Doing so makes it manageable. But in bite-sizing our approach, are we precluding the radical nature of partnership by enculturating it into the norm from the outset? Chapter 8 (Bell, Barahona, and Stanway) reminds us of the fluidity of partnership, that our roles/selves can change across time and contexts, and we thus suggest that the labelling of partnerships as discrete projects be approached with caution and further problematised in the future.

Students as Legitimate Author(itie)s

This collection—authored both solely and collaboratively by ~50% students—enacts a direct challenge to those who say, "But what would students know about teaching and learning?" There is still a pervasive fallacy that students' perspectives are valuable as data alone, which perpetuates a problematic trend where staff remain responsible for improving "the student experience." Hooks (1989, 42) states that a dimension of oppression is that

> those who dominate are seen as subjects and those who are dominated objects. As subjects, people have the right to define their own reality, establish their own identities, name their history. As objects, one's reality is defined by others, one's

identity created by others, one's history named only in ways that define one's relationship to those who are subject.

We are troubled to see that most often, students are positioned as objects in higher education (Felten et al. 2019).

This subject-object dichotomy is one we see reflected in publishing patterns on partnership. For example, recent research found that, of an analyzed set of articles on students as partners, 89% had a staff first author and 99% included staff authors more broadly. Meanwhile only a third included a student co-author—indicating a scarcity of student-led or solely student-authored articles in this space (Mercer-Mapstone et al. 2017). We are not implying that staff should not author work on students' experiences; those perspectives are as valuable as any other, and diverse perspectives on a complex issue—and dialogues among those perspectives as shown in this book—are generative. The issue here is, now that student perspectives are being seen as relevant to enhancing higher education, students face a struggle to make *themselves* heard and staff perspectives remain *the authority* on students' experiences. A resulting issue of this trend is highlighted by Wilson et al. in chapter 2 as students, even when they do author their own voices—such as in conference environments— still bear the burden of justification in terms of legitimizing their own voices and presence.

This collection shows that students can be seen as legitimate authors and authorities on their higher education experiences. We argue that this should increasingly be the case and that, often, students are better qualified than anyone else to speak to and author their own situated experiences. As an implication of this collection, we encourage readers to consider how to support students in taking up their agency to speak for themselves and author their own experiences.

Resourcing for Different Kinds of "Impact" and "Success"

Chapter 5 (Lenihan-Ikin et al.) shares: "Civic engagement *needs adequate resourcing*: / these initiatives require more investment than traditional courses . . . / there was an assumption that / a student would want to do this for free . . ." Resourcing partnership is a constant struggle. In workshops internationally, we constantly hear the question, "Yes, but where do I get the money?"

There are often (although not always) pots of money around, but equally as often, these pots get channeled toward initiatives that are *seen* to have wider impact. As a community of practitioners, we need to learn to position and communicate partnership in ways that both align with broader discourses and engage senior leaders in reconsidering what counts as impact or success. The question of success is taken up in Chapter 14 (Fraser et al.)—challenging the common outcomes-driven notion of success—and Chapter 12 (Narayanan and Abbot) reminds us to question the scale of impact we consider valuable in partnership contexts: "While this is a small sample in formal terms, it's huge for those four students who were so inspired in that first class they decided to make this their disciplinary home." What makes partnership valuable, then, may not necessarily be at huge scale but can be deeply transformational for individuals—especially those from marginalized backgrounds, as discussed in Chapters 2, 9, 10, and 12—and this is a critical consideration when weighing up how we resource and measure such initiatives. Such considerations become increasingly relevant as the student experience becomes a strategic priority in higher education. Highlighting that the outcomes of partnership (such as employability, transferable skills, engagement in learning, academic success, and metacognitive learning to name a few) align with measures of success which are traditionally valued in higher education will be an important part of positioning partnership as central to these broader discourses. In the risky context of increasing neoliberalism, we walk the fine line of also being clear that partnership challenges *how* those outcomes are achieved. These are discussions we need to be having with our bosses, managers, and senior leaders to make the case that partnership has benefits for individuals, groups, and institutions—but that it takes a new perspective to see (and resource) that value.

Openings

"Conclusions suggests an ending, a linear progression that can be resolved in some neat way. I see no conclusions here, but rather *openings*" (Glesne 1997, 218). We echo this sentiment with a final question for you in finishing this collection: What new openings do you now see in your life for partnership?

References

Carnevale, Anthony P., and Jeff Strohl. 2013. *Separate and Unequal: How Higher Education Reinforces the Intergenerational Reproduction of White Racial Privilege.* Washington, DC: Georgetown Public Policy Institute. https://cew.georgetown.edu/cew-reports/separate-unequal/.

Eddo-Lodge, Reni. 2017. *Why I'm No Longer Talking to White People About Race.* London: Bloomsbury Publishing PLC.

Felten, Peter. 2017. "Emotion and Partnership." *International Journal for Students as Partners* 1 (2): 1-9. https://doi.org/10.15173/ijsap.v1i2.3070.

Felten, Peter, Sophia Abbot, Jordan Kirkwood, Aaron Long, Tanya Lubicz-Nawrocka, Lucy Mercer-Mapstone, and Roselynn Verwoord. 2019. "Reimagining the Place of Students in Academic Development." *International Journal for Academic Development* 24 (2): 192-203. https://doi.org/10.1080/1360144X.2019.1594235.

Glesne, Corinne. 1997. "That Rare Feeling: Re-presenting Research Through Poetic Transcription." *Qualitative Inquiry* 3 (2): 202-21. https://doi.org/10.1177/107780049700300204.

Hermsen, Tara, Thomas Kuiper, Frits Roelofs, and Joost van Wijchen. 2017. "Without Emotions, Never a Partnership!" *International Journal for Students as Partners* 1 (2). https://doi.org/10.15173/ijsap.v1i2.3228.

hooks, bell. 1989. *Talking Back: Thinking Feminist, Thinking Black.* London: Sheba Feminist.

Mercer-Mapstone, Lucy, and Catherine Bovill. 2019. "Equity and Diversity in Institutional Approaches to Student-Staff Partnership Schemes in Higher Education." *Studies in Higher Education*: 1-17. https://doi.org/10.1080/03075079.2019.1620721.

Mercer-Mapstone, Lucy, Sam Lucie Dvorakova, Kelly E. Matthews, Sophia Abbot, Breagh Cheng, Peter Felten, Kris Knorr, Elizabeth Marquis, Rafaella Shammas, and Kelly Swaim. 2017. "A Systematic Literature Review of Students as Partners in Higher Education." *International Journal for Students as Partners* 1 (1): 1-23. https://doi.org/10.15173/ijsap.v1i1.3119.

ABOUT THE AUTHORS

Sophia Abbot is a graduate student in higher education at Elon University and got her start in this field as an undergraduate in Bryn Mawr College's SaLT program, where she developed an insatiable quest to spread partnership as a process and experience throughout higher education.

Anita Acai is a PhD candidate in psychology and health professions education at McMaster University in Hamilton, Ontario, Canada. Her research interests centre on understanding how principles of social and cognitive psychology can be applied to improve training for physicians, surgeons, and other health professionals. She also maintains an active interest in the scholarship of teaching and learning.

Mayed Ahmed is a biomedical scientist. He graduated with an honours degree in biomedical sciences from the University of Westminster in 2018. During the course of his undergraduate studies, Mayed conducted multiple co-creators projects with a focus on enhancing library services by developing a mobile application.

Stephanie Barahona is an honours candidate in the Department of History at the University of Sydney. During her undergraduate studies, she worked with Amani Bell to produce and present original research on students as partners in higher education. Stephanie's interest in higher education research is based on her passion to make universities more accessible and inclusive.

Ashley Beathe is a 21C student curriculum partner and studying a masters in education (secondary teaching) at Western Sydney University following degrees in arts and health sciences. She also works part-time in the Student Experience Office at the university.

Gulshanara (Rumy) Begum is senior lecturer in nutrition and exercise science at the University of Westminster. She has been teaching in higher education for over fifteen years and has a strong drive to help students realise the remarkable work that they are capable of and build a strong foundation for career aspirations.

Amani Bell's research takes a participatory approach to exploring the challenges and opportunities of higher education. She is lead editor of the book *Understanding Experiences of First Generation University Students: Culturally Responsive and Sustaining Methodologies,* published by Bloomsbury in 2018.

Stephen Bloch-Schulman was the inaugural winner (2017) of the Prize for Excellence in Philosophy Teaching, awarded by the American Philosophical Association, the American Association of Philosophy Teachers, and the Teaching Philosophy Association. He is an associate editor of Teaching and Learning Inquiry and is co-authoring *Thinking Through Questions* (forthcoming, Hackett Publishing) with Anthony Weston.

Anne Bruder is an associate professor of English at Berea College. She teaches and writes about nineteenth- and early twentieth-century American literature and culture, and experimental pedagogy. Her scholarship has appeared in, among other places, the *New England Quarterly*, the *Michigan Historical Review*, and *Literature in Transition*.

Nancy Chick is the director of faculty development at Rollins College (Florida, United States), editor of *SoTL in Action* (2018), co-editor of two Exploring Signature Pedagogies books (2009, 2012), and founding co-editor of *Teaching & Learning Inquiry*, the journal of the International Society for the Scholarship of Teaching and Learning (ISSOTL).

Alison Cook-Sather has developed internationally recognized programs that position students as pedagogical consultants to prospective secondary teachers and to practicing college faculty members. She has worked with hundreds of faculty and students participating in pedagogical partnership and co-created courses with students. She has published five books and over 100 articles and chapters on this and related work, many co-authored with student partners.

Anna Dolidze obtained a first class business management and marketing degree at the University of Westminster in 2018 due to her hard work, extra effort, and determination. Anna is passionate about behavioural psychology, qualitative research, and marketing. Her hobbies include cooking, writing, and photography.

Bradley Elliott is lecturer in physiology and Translational Physiology Research Group leader, University of Westminster. His research examines how muscle cells age, attempting to better understand how and why humans grow older. He also has a secondary interest in physiology teaching and technology driven learning.

Peter Felten's research focuses on the influence of human relationships, and on individual and institutional change, in undergraduate education. His books include *The Undergraduate Experience* (2016) and *Engaging Students as Partners in Learning and Teaching* (2014). He is co-editor of the *International Journal for Academic Development* and a fellow of the Gardner Institute.

Abbi Flint is an independent educational developer and researcher with longstanding interest and expertise in student engagement and partnership. She is a principal fellow of the Higher Education Academy and was a visiting research fellow in student engagement at Birmingham City University (2014-17). Abbi is particularly interested in how concepts of student engagement and partnership play out in practice, and how developing joint learning communities of students and staff can strengthen and sustain partnerships. Abbi's poems on other topics have been published in *Route 57*, and as part of the *Call and Response* project.

Jennifer Fraser is principal lecturer in the School of Social Sciences and university director of student partnership at the University of Westminster. Jennifer's academic background is in narrative and cultural theory, with work shaped by a commitment to inclusive practice and social justice. Jennifer is a National Teaching Fellow and a founding member of the Critical Pedagogies Group.

Hannah Goddard is a student engagement professional working within The Student Engagement Partnership (TSEP) at the National Union of Students. Hannah specialises in student engagement in higher education, focusing on student voice processes including student academic representation systems.

Rachel Guitman was an undergraduate student at the time this chapter was written, and as of spring 2019, has graduated from McMaster University with an honours bachelor of arts and science degree. As an interdisciplinary scholar, her research interests are varied, with main areas of interest being in philosophy of technology and science, medical history, cultural studies, and the scholarship of teaching and learning.

Sam Hester is an indie comics creator based in Calgary, Canada, and has always been interested in integrating comics and academic writing. As a professional graphic recorder who has collaborated with a wide range of organizations in Canada, Sam captures visual stories by drawing upon deep listening skills, a unique graphic style, a passion for community-building . . . and a lot of markers.

Chng Huang Hoon is an associate professor (English language) and is concurrently an associate provost (undergraduate education) and director (Chua Thian Poh Community Leadership Centre) at the National University of Singapore (NUS). She has degrees in linguistics (UT-Austin) and philosophy (NUS). She has served on the ISSOTL Board of Directors as regional vice president (Asia Pacific, 2017-2019), and is ISSOTL's co-president-elect (2019, with Nancy Chick).

Chinnu Jose is a third year bachelor of law/ bachelor of business (accounting) student at Western Sydney University, a 21C student curriculum partner, and is one of the student representatives on the University's Senate Education Committee.

Isabella Lenihan-Ikin is in her fifth year of a conjoint degree, bachelor of law and bachelor of science (hons), at Victoria University of

Wellington. Alongside her studies, Isabella is a student representative—she is a current student-member on the University Council and is a former vice president of the Students' Association.

Claire Lockard is a graduate student working on her PhD in philosophy. She is interested primarily in feminist philosophy and critical race theory, and she is working on a dissertation about the ways that the call for interpretative charity in academic philosophy can enact epistemic harm on already-marginalized philosophers.

Racquel Lynch is a former 21C student curriculum partner at Western Sydney University who was, at the time, studying medical science. She has now left student life to pursue new business opportunities.

Evgeniya Macleod is a senior lecturer at Westminster Business School (WBS), University of Westminster, London, UK. As a course leader Evgeniya is passionate about student learning experience and well-being. As a teacher who values student voice she has supported "Students as Co-Creators" projects at WBS as an academic partner.

Marisse Manthos is in her final semester of a bachelor of arts majoring in English and will move into the masters of education (secondary teaching) at Western Sydney University. She is a 21C student curriculum partner and a 2018-2019 summer scholarship student working on the research project "Teach the University."

Jenny Marie oversees a range of educational enhancement work, including University College London's student partnership schemes: UCL ChangeMakers, which supports enhancement projects; and Student Quality Reviewers, which supports student participation in quality assurance processes. She loves reading fiction and is interested in how the narratives we tell affect our lives.

Elizabeth Marquis is an assistant professor in the Arts & Science Program at McMaster University and associate director (research) at the university's teaching and learning institute. Beth's SoTL research focuses on the intersections between teaching and learning and questions of equity and justice, and on film as public pedagogy. She's also committed to supporting and researching student-faculty partnerships and oversees McMaster's Student Partners Program.

Sasha Mathrani has worked in partnership with faculty members at both Haverford and Bryn Mawr Colleges. She also facilitated a cohort of student partners focused on implementing the principles of "Universal Design for Learning," and co-led a workshop on inclusive teaching that was open to all faculty at Haverford and Bryn Mawr. After graduating from Haverford, she began work at St. Luke's School in New Canaan, Connecticut, where she works as an academic technologist to help faculty enhance teaching and learning through technology.

Kelly E. Matthews is currently an academic (member of faculty) at the University of Queensland, Brisbane, Australia.

Susannah McGowan focuses most of her daily work on designing and implementing evidence-based educational development programs for faculty, professional staff, and students as a vehicle for curricular transformation. Her research interests include digital, threshold concepts in history, student as partners work, and the impact of educational development in higher education. Susannah is also a Gardner Institute fellow and she co-facilitates the Teaching and Learning Academy, an annual course design workshop incorporating inclusive, evidence-based pedagogies.

Lucy Mercer-Mapstone was a postgraduate student when this book was in its infancy. When the book was published, she was a lecturer in higher education pedagogy. Her research and practice focus on student engagement and social justice in higher education teaching and learning.

Helen Meskhidze is a graduate student at the University of California, Irvine. Her research focuses on epistemological issues that arise in astrophysics and cosmology. She is particularly interested in the roles computer simulations play in such contexts.

Desika Narayanan is an assistant professor of astronomy at the University of Florida, though was an assistant professor of physics and astronomy at Haverford College during his time of student-teacher partnership with Sophia Abbot. Alongside his research interests of theoretical galaxy evolution and star formation, he is interested in increasing the accessibility of the field to a more diverse student and researcher population.

Kathy Nguyen is studying science at Western Sydney University and is a former 21C student curriculum partner. She is currently working in the university's Graduate Research School.

Anita Ntem graduated from Bryn Mawr College in 2018 with a degree in psychology and a minor in educational studies. Her journey in student-faculty partnerships through the Students as Learners and Teachers (SaLT) program afforded her the opportunity to engage in various departmental partnerships, lead consultant meetings, and become a presenter and facilitator for partnership conferences, resulting in her continued efforts in academia.

Brad Olsen is a senior economist at Infometrics and a community leader. During his studies, Brad was a student representative on the Academic Board and the Faculty of Commerce Board. In 2016, he was named as New Zealand's Queen's Young Leader for his leadership and youth engagement work.

Tai Peseta is a senior lecturer in the Learning Transformations team at Western Sydney University. She leads the student partnership strategy as part of the University's 21C Project.

Julie Phillips graduated from Elon University in 2015 with a BA in history and international studies, and a minor in political science. She earned her JD from William & Mary Law School in 2019 and is currently practicing in Washington, D.C.

Jenny Pizzica is a senior lecturer in the Learning Transformations team at Western Sydney University. She leads the university's 21C strategy on partnership pedagogy.

Hassan Raza is a 21C student curriculum partner and is nearing the end of his study in business, marketing, and arts at Western Sydney University. He also works casually in the Student Experience Office at the university.

Heather Smith is professor of global and international studies at the University of Northern British Columbia. Currently on leave, she is a visiting scholar in the Department of Political Science at Dalhousie University. She is also a 3M National Teaching Fellow (2006).

Bonnie Rose Stanway conducts doctoral research at the University of Sydney, exploring the intersection of sociolinguistics, cultural competence, and organisational studies. She is also a passionate educator, as a tutor and an associate lecturer in the Business School. Bonnie is focussed on improving policies and practices which encourage the success of both international and domestic students.

Kathryn Sutherland is an associate professor in the Centre for Academic Development. Her research and teaching focus on early career academics, and more recently, on student-staff partnerships in learning and teaching. She is co-director of Victoria University of Wellington's new partnership programme, Ako in Action.

Emma Tennent is a PhD student in psychology, studying language and social interaction, with a focus on gender and identity. She is new to the work of academic development, but excited to further explore the possibilities of partnership in learning and teaching.

Kate Carruthers Thomas is senior research fellow at Birmingham City University, specialising in interdisciplinary research into higher education, gender, and equalities. She classes herself as an accidental cartoonist and is developing a practice of graphic social science, using visual methods and media in her research practice and communication.

Moonisah Usman is a PhD candidate in biomedical sciences and the student partnership programme coordinator at the University of Westminster. Moonisah has an interest in inclusive pedagogical practices that crosses both her disciplinary and partnership work. Moonisah's research and teaching is in the area of physiology, molecular genetics, and cancer.

Roselynn Verwoord is a PhD candidate in the Department of Educational Studies at the University of British Columbia (UBC). She works as a curriculum consultant at the UBC Centre for Teaching Learning and

Technology and as an instructor in teacher education and adult education. Her research interests include student partnership and teacher inquiry.

Marc Wilson, as well as teaching and researching social psychology, mental health, and psychological research methods and statistics, has been involved in scholarship around learning and teaching that has included (following behind Kathryn Sutherland) early career academic experiences, the experiences of departmental heads, and initiatives fostering Maori and Pasifika student success.

Sean Wilson is currently completing his master's of arts in teaching at Duke University. He plans to teach social studies in Durham public schools beginning in August 2019.

Fathimath Zuruwath Zareer is a third-year undergraduate studying accounting at the University of Westminster and is currently interning on a finance industrial placement at Goldman Sachs. Zuruwath was part of a research group on career and employability services and also sits on the course committee panel. She spends her free time travelling, fashion designing, and reading.

INDEX

Printed in Great Britain
by Amazon

43434305R00148